Servant Leadership

Volume 4

Leaving a Legacy

Rocky Wallace

ROWMAN & LITTLEFIELD EDUCATION
A division of
ROWMAN & LITTLEFIELD PUBLISHERS, INC.
Lanham • New York • Toronto • Plymouth, UK

Published by Rowman & Littlefield Education
A division of Rowman & Littlefield Publishers, Inc.
A wholly owned subsidary of The Rowman & Littlefield Publishing Group, Inc.
4501 Forbes Boulevard, Suite 200, Lanham, Maryland 20706
http://www.rowmaneducation.com

Estover Road, Plymouth PL6 7PY, United Kingdom

British Library Cataloguing in Publication Information Available

Library of Congress Cataloging-in-Publication Data

Library of Congress Cataloging-in-Publication Data Available
ISBN 978-1-61048-634-7 (cloth : alk. paper) — ISBN 978-1-61048-635-4 (pbk. : alk. paper) — ISBN 978-1-61048-636-1 (electronic)

©™ The paper used in this publication meets the minimum requirements of American National Standard for Information Sciences Permanence of Paper for Printed Library Materials, ANSI/NISO Z39.48-1992.

Printed in the United States of America

I dedicate this book to my students. Their array of talents and devotion to the calling of teaching inspires me to keep writing about what effective schools of the future can be.

Contents

Foreword

Servant Leadership is needed in all facets of life!

I have spent a great deal of time studying servant leadership over the many years, and the one thing I am convinced of is the great need we have of it; in our lives, in our homes, in our workplaces, in our communities, in our societies, and in our world. I am also convinced of this, that each of us can be a servant leader, there is no limitation on this type of leading just as there is no limitation on leading with love, or as Robert K. Greenleaf said—this type of love has "unlimited liability."

Dr. Rocky Wallace is a graduate of our doctoral programs here at Regent University, as well, he has attended our annual Servant Leadership Research Roundtable. The one compelling aspect of the roundtables is the telling of the stories of servant leadership—be it from the far away corners of the world or the neighbor beside us every day.

I congratulate Dr. Wallace on this beautiful addition to the servant leadership literature, what a valuable addition it is. The mixture of stories, lessons, application and reflection provide a great depth for the reader. Not only is one compelled to think about servant leadership, one is compelled to act on it and consider the possibilities—that are indeed grand and noble. I hope as you read, and consider your own leadership journey, that you would embrace the idea of servant leadership and make it you're life-calling, for indeed it is greater to serve.

Kathleen Patterson, Ph.D.
Associate Professor
School of Global Leadership and Entrepreneurship
Regent University

Preface

In continuing this series on principal mentoring, I am reminded by my graduate students that we often fail to do enough discussion about the real world of school leadership. In reality, a principal's day is about the array of relationships that make up the school community, and how well the staff understands the principle of authentic love and care for students. When a culture of a healthy one-to-one relationship is emphasized as a non-negotiable core value, then magical things will begin to happen as the artificial "structures" of school transform into mentors and their pupils learning and growing together.

In this story, John, the wise mentor, has become seriously ill. As he coaches Brad through another year, it is evident that he is sharing much more than how to meet the demands of running a school. He is extending to Brad a blessing. He is now seeing his world through a different lens, and uses every opportunity to help Brad understand the long view—the bigger picture of how fragile life is, and how we must create wonderfully stimulating and supportive opportunities for our students who are entrusted to our care.

Through John's intense battle, we join his masterful weaving of lessons that provide a glimpse into what the "schools of the future" could be, and should be. These innovative, creative, social communities will have the potential to transform society and will not have the bureaucratic, impersonal, rigid structures that have plagued schooling for decades. Instead, they will support and inspire all students as well as staff to thirst for learning and lifetime growing that then gives back in such positive ways to society.

After all, isn't this what we have hoped schools would be all along?

Acknowledgments

I am forever grateful to Dr. Tom Koerner, and his fine team, for how they provide such professional and friendly support on my writing projects.

I am also grateful to the colleagues I work with every day, who are so committed to diving into the research and helping our teachers in the trenches to be expert practitioners—always focused on what's best for kids and school improvement.

And, as always, I am blessed to have a wife who is totally supportive of my career and other life endeavors. Denise's steady love and devotion inspires me to do visionary work. She is such a wise mentor to me and so many others.

Chapter One

Intersections

One never knows when the journey will take a sudden turn. And on that day, it is then that we know just how well we've lived our life. No one has to spell out for us this or that. No one has to remind us of anything at all. It's all right in front of us, clear as a bell. On that day, for some folks for the first time . . . our eyes are wide open.

Life lesson: When our work is done, our legacy depends on how well we empowered and mentored others to stand in the gap and keep the vision alive.

John's mind was in another place as he drove home from the doctor's office. In fact, it was almost like time had stopped. He felt surreal, as if he weren't even driving his car. His life flashed before his eyes, and he longed to be with his wife and kids right then. He longed to be with them somewhere, anywhere—where he was safe and warm. But today, for the first time ever, he had realized that he may never feel such security again. He may never feel the serenity of a "hiding place" in the same way he had felt it before. For today, his doctor had shared with him that he had cancer . . . the very serious kind . . . life threatening . . . possibly terminal.

As he tried to stay focused on the road, while wiping tears from his eyes, John thought about the principal mentoring project that he had grown over the last three years. Last year, it had been developed as a state model. This coming year, it was being expanded to other states. Who would he give this wonderful responsibility to? Who would keep the project going? He knew he had a long evening ahead of him at home, as his family would be shocked and heartbroken. They would need his undivided attention. So, the next thing he knew, his pickup was pulling into Smith School.

John had mentored Brad and his assistant, Millie, during the last school year, and had been so impressed with their leadership as they helped this little P–12 school rise from the ashes of a fire. Now it had become a model being emulated around the state and country as an authentic, relationship-focused, state-of-the-art learning center. Brad's staff and the Smithtown community had returned the original meaning of "school" to the classroom where it belongs—with the teacher and the pupil. And Smithtown had embraced the school with the love and support that had made all the difference.

As John broke the news to Brad, the two embraced in a long hug that was graced simply by a hush and sobs. Finally, with trembling and broken voice, Brad interrupted the silence.

"John, we'll help you beat this. You know how doctors are. They have to explain the worst-case scenario first, but then, often, it's not near as bad as it sounds."

"Brad, son, sit down and let's talk. This is reality, not simply a doctor's caution. I started losing my energy in the spring, and began losing weight at the beginning of the summer. They've run all kinds of tests. What I have is a fast-growing kind, and it has already spread. I'm going to take chemotherapy, and do everything I can to get well. But I must be honest with you . . . it doesn't look good. What I came by to ask you was—would you consider taking the principal mentoring program this year?"

Brad's eyes fell to the floor, and he could not say anything for several seconds. "John, I don't know what to say. I was so looking forward to you mentoring me again, and also going to your monthly leadership cadre sessions."

"Well, you can still do that—but on the coaching end of it perhaps. You know how to build a great school, Brad. You know what it takes in getting back to relationship, and what kids need, and how to involve the entire community. I saw you turn it around here at Smith School in one year! To be honest, I was amazed."

"John, if you really need me for a while to help on this, I'd love to do it. But how?"

"If Millie could run this school, I'm sure Dr. Cobb would let you step away for at least a few months to further develop this program. There are state meetings you will need to attend, and ones on the national level as well. Plus, there are more principals in the region who you would be mentoring, one to one, just as I have been doing."

"But who would mentor me, John?" Brad's voice broke again.

"I would."

Brad looked up with a sudden hope in his eyes. "You?"

"Yes. At my home. Instead of me driving down here, you can visit me in my home every couple of weeks, and we can talk about anything you want to as you take on the role of the coordinator of the principal mentoring project."

"You would do that for me, John?"

"You bet I would, Brad. In fact, it would be an honor. After all, passing the torch to my successor is a critical role I will need to play. The principal's network is getting bigger, and bigger, and bigger. We must not drop the ball on this. Why not now, while there is still time? And why not with you? I can't think of someone more well suited for the job."

"Should we go talk to Dr. Cobb? Because if he'll let me do this, I'm in. I'm humbled that you thought of me, John. I'll do it."

John smiled, and put his hat on. "*You* go talk to Dr. Cobb, Brad. . . . It's best that you let him know personally that you want to do this. Tell him I'll visit him in the morning with the details of my illness, and with how I recommend we proceed with the project. Right now, I need to go home to my family. I'll sleep better tonight now, Brad. Thank you."

In Effective Succession Planning, *Rothwell (2005) stresses the critical importance of empowering and equipping within so the good work continues after leadership has moved on.*

SUMMARY

John is given the shocking news that he has malignant cancer, and asks Brad to take over his principal mentoring program, which is now expanding to a national project. Brad agrees, but desires to keep John as his mentor. John suggests that Brad visit him at home regularly during the next few months so they can keep their one-to-one chats going.

REFLECTION

1. Have you ever been faced with a serious illness in your family, or with a close friend?
2. What changes in the relationship?
3. Does your school or district have an effective succession plan in place?

Chapter Two

Moments in Time

One's journey should be filled with wonderful memories . . . highlights of a life well lived. If we so mismanage or disregard our time that we can't remember an abundance of "smiles," then we haven't lived much at all.

Life lesson: Leading is about authentic, caring relationships.

Brad walked slowly up the walk to John's front door. He didn't know if this was such a good idea, but John had requested it, so he would oblige. Before he could knock, the door swung open and there was Marge, John's wife, with swollen eyes but a welcoming smile on her face.

"Brad, I am so glad you came. John has been telling me about your arrangement this year. Instead of him coming to your school, you're coming here. He is so, so excited about this. I can't tell you how much this mentoring program means to him, and your willingness to help until he gets better is such a blessing."

Brad hugged Marge, comforted by her anticipation that John would get better—exactly what he needed to hear. "Marge, I am honored to do it. I just don't want to barge in while John's taking his treatments and resting. You always call when he's not able to see me."

"I will, Brad. That's so thoughtful of you. But I can tell you, I doubt John will want to cancel many of these. He got up extra early this morning knowing you were coming. He can't wait to get started."

As Brad made his way into John's den, he was struck by the warmth of this home. Pictures of John and Marge and their kids were everywhere, and John's love of the outdoors was evident as art work of nature and photos of family vacations, fishing, and camping trips made each room look more like a museum.

"Brad, I've been waiting on you. How's it going with the new job?" John gave Brad a long hug as he stood up from reclining in his "lazy boy."

"Sit back down, John. I'll just sit here on the couch, and won't stay long this morning. I don't want to wear you out. Marge tells me you're doing great!"

"Well, the treatment has started, if that's what you mean. I'm starting to lose my hair, so if I keep my ball cap on when you come to visit this fall, you'll know why. Yes, I'm feeling reasonably well—just not getting to take my hikes like I usually do, so I miss being outdoors. But, the doctors say that later on that might be possible. For now—they just want me going one step at a time."

"You look good, John. Maybe you can attend one of our principal cadre sessions later on when the doctor says you're ready. I met with the gang last week, and they all send their best, and are praying for you. . . . Man, we missed your touch. You don't know how good you are at leading a group in a heart-to-heart discussion."

"I'm sure you'll get the hang of it, Brad. Just follow your instincts. And remember, ask thoughtful questions, and then mainly just sit back and listen."

"Oh, I'm doing that part well. I've been assigned a first-year principal to mentor one-on-one, and he has that deer-in-the-headlights look these first few weeks on the job. I remember those days well myself. But, he won't open up much to me at all, John. I'll ask a question, he'll give a real short answer, and then we just sort of sit there."

John sat back in his recliner and chuckled. "Just be patient and be there for him, Brad. That's the main thing."

"What would you suggest I make sure he gets down pat this first semester? It seems he's overwhelmed with everything."

"Mainly, make sure he gets in touch with himself. Help him understand self-leadership. He'll never grasp the wonder of servant leadership until he can harness himself."

"Good point. I'll focus on that during the next few visits. In fact, I need to stress this with the cadre, too. Thanks, John—very helpful. . . . What else?"

"Tell him to laugh."

"Tell him to laugh?"

"Yeah—a lot."

"And just how do I get this point across, John? Principals are usually going a mile a minute, wearing many hats, and putting out fires everyday. We usually don't have lots of time to laugh."

"Then something's out of whack. Make sure he sees the faces all around him."

"The faces?"

"Yes, Brad—you know, the people. He'll be a great principal if he but does one thing well. And that one thing is to see his people through their eyes, and then have compassion, and lighten their day with a smile, a good joke, an air of support that lets them know he's proud of them, he believes in them, and that everything's going to be alright."

"What a powerful formula, John. And, I need to practice this more myself."

"Tell him the next time a teacher comes into the office with a complaint or an issue, to sit down, and take the time to find out what's really going on. Be her brother, so to speak—not simply her supervisor. And the next time a student gets sent to the office for discipline, tell him to do the same thing. Find out what's going on in that child's world, and then feel with compassion so that child knows he has a principal who cares—not just an authority figure who walks around the building all day long like a policeman at the mall."

"I will, John. I will convey this message to all the principals I work with this year."

"By the way, how's Millie doing as principal at Smith School while you're doing this project?"

"She's doing OK, John. You mentored her well last year, too, while you were helping me. But she's got some gray hair I didn't notice last year, and she's working awfully long hours. I do worry that over the long haul the job will heap way too much stress on her."

"Tell her ol' John says she's got to lighten up."

"I will. But you know Millie—she's not going to do it unless she gives one hundred and ten percent."

"But we can be giving one hundred and ten percent every day and still miss the point, Brad. Tell you what I'd like you to do. Give Millie an assignment for me, and then ask her to come by to see me in a few days."

"OK. What do you want me to tell her to do?"

"Pictures."

"Pictures?"

"Lots and lots of pictures."

"Help me out here, John. Pictures of what?"

"Tell Millie to simply walk around the school, at least one morning a week for a half hour or so, and take pictures of the smiling faces of Smith School. Take pictures of kids in class, in the labs, teachers teaching, lunch time, field trips, PE class, band practice, buses loading on rainy days, the secretary on the intercom . . . and so on. When the first semester is over, her only assignment from me this entire year is to put together a slide show to present to the entire school during Christmas week."

"You know Millie, John. Will she think she has the time to do this?"

"Brad, she doesn't have the time not to. I guarantee you—this will help Millie more than anything else we coach her on this year."

"I trust your instincts, John. I'll follow up on this. But I still fail to see the point."

"You need a camera, too."

"What? Me? Why?"

"So you can figure it out. Buy a camera for the mentoring program and take pictures of the principals you're working with one on one, your cadre, the schools you visit—take pictures even on your national trips you're taking to promote the program in other states. Make sure you've got that camera with you at all times, and use it at least two or three times a day."

"Sounds like a reasonable strategy I guess. And this will help me to . . . ?"

"See the smiling faces, and remember them. This year will not pass this way again, Brad. Next year, whether you're still mentoring, or back at the helm of a school—is next year. . . . This year only happens once. Don't get lost in the minutia of daily schedules, and checking items off your 'to do' list. Live this year, Brad. . . . Live it! . . . See into the hearts of the people that make up your life. Capture their smiles; treasure your relationships with them. Carpe diem! Seize the day! Not seize your list of projects to get done. Instead, cherish the precious people who you will meet and help each day, and who are the reason you get to serve in the role of an educator. You have one of the best jobs in the world, Brad. Any teacher or principal does. Take it and run with it, son. Take it and run with it! Savor the smiles; even savor the tears. And then you have figured out life, Brad. Then you have lived."

In Who Cares, *Kelly E. Middleton and Elizabeth A. Petitt (2007) illustrate how authentic customer service can take any school district to a higher level, as stakeholders are treated with respect and shown that they are valued.*

SUMMARY

Brad makes his first visit to John's home as he starts the semester in his new role as the coordinator of John's mentoring program. John shares with him key secrets about self-leadership and cherishing the people who make up our lives.

REFLECTION

1. How would you describe the culture of your school?
2. When one walks around your campus, is there an abundance of smiling faces, and people enjoying their work?

3. What changes need to be made to create a stronger relationship focus at your school?

Chapter Three

New Beginnings

Every person you meet is a unique and gifted individual . . . a one-of-a-kind who has hopes and dreams, hurts and failure, others who depend on them—just as you do.

Life lesson: Pictures tell rich stories of the people who make up the organization, and a *history* void of an array of recorded memories speaks volumes about the culture.

Millie sat down beside John's recliner and without saying a word, put her head in her hands and started sobbing.

"Sakes alive, little gal, what's wrong?" John reached for a tissue box and handed it to her.

"John, it's not fair for me to do this. You're sick, and that in itself has been a blow to me these first few weeks. We miss you so, so much down at the school. Your visits last year made all the difference in how Brad and I were able to help re-build Smith School. But we also miss you at the cadre sessions. The other principals send their best, and want you to come be with our group as soon as you can."

"I will do my best, Millie. I look forward to hopefully seeing everyone again soon. But let's not talk about me. I'm following doctor's orders, and resting right here at home just like he told me to. I'm reading some great books that I had been putting off, and writing some, too. So far, I'm doing OK. . . . But now the look in your eye, that's another story. What else is going on? Have you been taking pictures as I asked Brad to have you do?"

"Oh yes, John! And I am loving it! It's the best part of my day—walking around the school and finding folks engaged in their work. But . . ."

Millie reached in her purse for her handkerchief as she began crying again. "But what, Millie? Go ahead, take your time. Let it out. Tell me what's bothering you so."

"John, I am just so worried about one of our staff who is going through huge issues at home that I did not know about. I have been on her case pretty hard about not turning paperwork in on time, about coming in late for work, about not staying for after-school meetings. Then, yesterday, I happened to run into her husband at the grocery store after school, and come to find out, they're getting a divorce. They have three precious children who also attend our school, and I just feel like such a jerk."

"Millie, why would you feel that way? You didn't know your teacher was having such a hard time in her personal life."

"But, John, I should have known. I am her principal, her supervisor. We even traveled together to a conference this summer. What must she think of me in terms of someone she can go to with problems if she didn't even feel she could let me know about this?"

"Perhaps she didn't want anyone to know at school. Perhaps, Millie, she did not want to burden down the school with such a traumatic, painful issue."

"No, I have found out that others in the building knew. So, she must have just felt like it would be a nuisance to me, or either she doesn't really feel she can come to me as a friend . . . as someone who cares for her on a relationship level that runs much deeper than just the output she produces at school."

"Maybe she's right."

"What? John, you know me better than that. I love my school. I love the staff, the kids, their parents, the community."

"But Millie, listen to how you just phrased that. It sounds as if you love the concept of being part of such a successful partnership, as if that's all you have to do to maintain the momentum your staff built last year. After all, Smith School is a pretty outstanding place—known all over the state and beyond as a model center that other schools can be learning from. And you are to be commended for helping make that transformation take place. You're a huge reason for the Smith School success story. But, what about the space in between?"

"Space in between?"

"Yes, you know—the one-to-one relationships. The real-life issues. Your school is known as a relationship-driven school. Your community has embraced all of you because of that people factor that is such an important core value of Smith School. But in all the frenzy of now being visited by others who want to know more about your formula, and the typical busy-ness of starting another school year, have you perhaps lost some focus of the one-to-one needs of your staff?"

"Yes, John, I have."

"Then most likely your staff is losing that focus, too, in relating one-to-one with their students. It becomes a ripple effect—that's how organizational culture works. Tell me about your typical work day recently."

"Well, with Brad not there to help me, I just can't seem to stay caught up. I'm up to my eyeballs with state assessment paperwork. I'm filling in for our academic team coach, who just last week decided he was burned out and abruptly resigned on us. I have a PTA president who has delegated the fall festival to me this year—don't quite know how I let that one get dumped in my lap."

Millie shook her head. "And, I seem to have had more meetings at central office this year than ever before. Besides all of this and the other usual principal duties, it seems that this year the teachers are sending more discipline referrals to the office. I've been given that role, too, and I hate it. I'm not good with the problem kids. So, I assign them to after-school detention, and usher them out of my office as soon as possible. I don't like them, and they don't like me. And that's just fine with me if it stays that way."

"But Millie, listen to yourself. You're explaining your job as if it's consumed with responsibilities you don't even enjoy. That was not how you were sounding last year. Instead, you embraced your work. You saw Smith School as one of your life callings."

Millie lowered her head again, and whispered her words with brokenness. "I know, John. I know. . . . What's changed?"

"Well, for one thing, it sounds like you're letting others dump work on you on short notice. That's not fair to you, no matter what their reasons. The teacher who up and reneged on his academic team responsibilities after the season had started? I'd have a talk with him, and let him know he'll have to make it through this season, as he had committed to, and then you will find a replacement for him as soon as the last meet is completed. Perhaps even find a parent volunteer or two to assist him now. In regard to the fall festival, if the PTA has done it in the past, simply explain to their president that she will need to find volunteers to coordinate this project, as always. You can meet with them every couple of weeks to monitor their progress, and give them helpful ideas."

"You're right, John. I've taken on way too much, which is not empowering the people who need to be helping with these programs."

"And, it's keeping you from the other responsibilities that you have taken on, and need to facilitate well. . . . As to the discipline referrals, I think you'll see them go down if you will do two things. Meet with your teachers one-to-one in the next few days and get to know them again."

John paused, being careful to not appear agitated. "And, secondly, let them know you need their help in building a schoolwide discipline plan that is seamless. The best schools have such a strong culture in place that rarely do classroom teachers have to send students to the office for further correction. But, on the other hand, Millie, when kids do get sent to you for an infraction or other issue, they need to see that you care. They need to see your empathy. Let them talk, be a good listener, and build authentic relationships with them as one of their key role models in these, their most impressionable years."

"And that's what my teacher who's going through the divorce needs, too. Isn't it?"

"Yes, of course. It sounds like you've been so busy keeping your head above water, you're accidentally letting others drown. Quite a paradox, isn't it? But, it's true. When we spend all of our time just thrashing around, maybe even trying to do the work other able people should be doing, still other victims go under. Life is about helping where others can't, Millie. That's the secret. When your daily tasks prevent this, there has to be some restructuring somewhere."

"I know, I know. I had this all down pretty well last year, John. I don't know what happened over the summer."

"Don't be too hard on yourself, Millie. I'll tell you what happened over the summer. . . . *Life happened.* Brad is now doing my job for a while, so he's not there. And all of these examples you've shared with me of others feeling stressed so they've dumped responsibilities on you . . . this is life. Life for a school family is no different than life for a family at home. Issues happen. And that's where your core values have to be rock solid. As the key administrative leader in this school, one essential core value is for you to always have time for the one-to-one conversations and the building of deep, trusting relationships."

"I need to schedule time, perhaps every week, to really talk with and especially listen to my teacher who's going through the marriage issues. I bet she's so, so torn up inside right now. It's a wonder she's even able to come to school every day. She needs my support—not my criticism because she's not getting her paperwork done. Think about it, John—what's all that *stuff* we make her do mean to her now? Her home's falling apart!"

"She'll cherish you doing this, Millie. Just be there for her. She may even need a day off, or a week. She and her husband need to see a counselor if they're not doing so already, and take a month just to sort everything out— maybe even a month off work. In reality, their kids, their family, their future together . . . it all sort of weighs in the balance right now."

"I also need to take the time to talk to my academic coach, don't I, and find out what's really going on in his life that has him feeling so burned out."

"Yes."

"I need to talk to my PTA president, don't I, and try to understand better the pressures she's feeling in that position."

"Yes."

"And I probably need to talk to Brad, my supervisor last year and the head principal last year. He could help me with a lot of this stuff if he knew more in detail what was going on with me emotionally on the inside."

"Yes."

"And I guess it couldn't hurt to talk to Dr. Cobb, and let him know that even though we have such a small school, with only a hundred and fifty kids or so, I need him to think about giving me an assistant principal, at least part-time."

"Yes."

"It really is all about relationship, isn't it, John?"

"That's all there is, Millie. In a nutshell, it's the essence of this human journey. Don't miss it, Millie. Don't miss it."

In The Power of Less, *Leo Babauta (2009) shares practical strategies for getting unnecessary tasks out of our daily lives, so we are free for the more important.*

SUMMARY

Millie pays a visit to John's home, and unloads her frustrations as the new school year finds her overwhelmed. John reminds her that she must clear her plate of added distractions that are keeping her from her real work—supportive, trusting relationships with her staff and students.

REFLECTIONS

1. What is the process in your school for coming to the aid of a student or staff person who is having debilitating private-life issues, or is this left to the school counselor(s) to take care of?
2. Has your staff had professional development in the area of emotional intelligence and authentic relationships?
3. Does your school make time to celebrate with slide shows, photo displays around the building, or other ways of keeping the focus on the variety of interesting people who make up your school?

Chapter Four

Careers and Life Callings

The one man worked, but only to survive . . . tired, uninspired, not feeling appreciated. The other man seized his passions when he was a boy and never let go. He didn't really see his work as drudgery. Instead, he drank from it as if it were the fountain of his very life.

Life lesson: When a child leaves high school unfulfilled, what does that say about the "system" that was supposed to prepare him for a life of purpose and dreams?

"Come on, John, we're going for a drive." Brad was dressed in his jeans, a t-shirt, hiking boots, and a ball cap.

John was surprised and looked at Marge for permission. She nodded in agreement with a gentle smile on her face. "The doctor says it's OK, Honey. I called him this morning to make sure."

"Where are we going, Brad?"

"I'm taking you to a backwoods trail and waterfall on a farm the next county over. I don't think you've ever been there, and you'll love it, John. It's absolutely beautiful."

"Then what are we waiting for? Let's go!"

Within an hour, John and Brad were sitting in a meadow looking at one of the prettiest little hideaways of nature that John had ever seen. In all of his years of hiking the trails of his home region, he had never found this particular spot.

"It's breathtaking, Brad."

"I know. One of our students told me about it. His grandfather owns several acres back in here, and very rarely does he give anyone permission to explore it."

"I have missed my hikes, Brad. Maybe my doctor will let me keep doing this. I *so* need it."

"Perhaps he'd let you if Marge came with you."

"That would be priceless. I'll ask her to check on this for me. The doctors want me exercising, but not getting run down and catching a cold. But, this makes me stronger! I feel more alive this morning than I have in a long time."

"John, you always seem on top of your game to me. I've never known a person who enjoys life more . . . all of it."

"I've always been blessed, Brad, with the joy of work. I can't remember not enjoying what I do as a vocation."

"And that's no doubt helped you enjoy the other parts of life—marriage, your kids, your hobbies, getting out in nature like this."

"Sure it has. It all ties together. My dad always told me: 'John, when you find your passion, God's call on your life—what you're good at and what serves humanity so you leave it a better place than when you found it—then Son, you have lived.'"

"What wisdom your father had, John. He was so right. When our work is interesting and meaningful, and in a passion zone, it's almost not even like work. It becomes something we can get up to every morning and go do with satisfaction—not dread or resentment. . . . And this is one thing that bothers me a lot about some of our kids down at our school. Too many of our seniors don't seem to have a clue about what they want to do with their life once they graduate."

"It's because they have yet to grasp a vision, Brad."

"A vision? High schoolers?"

"Yes, they're ready by that age to be setting bold goals for their lives. But sadly, we've too often saddled them down with these formalized rites of passage that leave them shaking their heads and wanting something just the opposite of what they need next in their journey."

"How do you mean, John?"

"What I'm saying is simply this: School is our one chance to equip the next generation to live lives of purpose . . . fulfilling lives that they will enjoy, and that will also give back to society. Surely, in the thirteen or fourteen years we have them, we can get them ready—all of them."

"But, John, what else can we do? Our upperclassmen are already taking so many courses, and are involved in more projects and extracurriculars than ever before. I think our school does a really good job in this area."

"You do, Brad—one of the most varied menu of services for students I've seen anywhere."

"Then what else can we do? It's as if the kids just assume life's going to be handed to them on a silver platter. It's as if they don't have any foresight. Is that how they see the rest of us? That we just sort of lucked out and landed on our feet with great careers?"

"Talk to them."

"What?"

"Talk to them, Brad. Especially in a small school like yours, you all have such a golden opportunity to mentor these kids as they transition from high school during their last couple of years."

"You mean more than just getting to know them in the hallways, and at ballgames, don't you?"

"Yes, I mean you suggest in your mentoring with Millie that she as the principal schedule one-to-one meetings with every junior and senior at Smith School, and have heart-to-heart talks about their passions, their interests, where they might want to shadow in a career setting or volunteer hours as a service project. Ask them what colleges they would like to visit, and then set those visits up for them. Make sure someone from the school community takes them if their parents can't, or won't. With Millie and her guidance counselor helping, and the high school faculty getting plugged in wherever she needs them to assist, I promise you, you all will see a significant increase in your kids leaving Smith School with a vision and on a mission."

"Don't get me wrong, John. I like your ideas, and it all sounds so perfect in theory. But in real life, this mindset would really need to be embraced throughout the school on all grade levels, not just senior high."

"Absolutely. Then do it."

"And honestly, sometimes the biggest obstacle is the parents and their seemingly lack of interest, or their not knowing how to fill out the paperwork for scholarships, college applications, and so on."

"Oh, you're right again, Brad. You would have to bring the parents into these discussions early on. In fact, they would need to sit in with their child and the school counselor and make commitments to the steps that you all would be helping the students to develop."

"John, I've been around you long enough to know that you've just created another job for me to do!" John then skipped a rock across the water. "But, I like it. It's time we stopped expecting teenagers to figure all of this stuff out. How can they have vision for their lives if they don't even know what the word means?"

"They'll still have to navigate through some choppy waters, Brad. And some will change schools, change majors; others will go other postsecondary routes—perhaps the military, or trade school. But that's the whole point. The Smith School staff and community will have been supporting them, guiding them, pushing doors open for them so they do have a plan. Certainly a better strategy than just turning them loose on graduation night and hoping for the best. That's what too many schools have done for too long and it hasn't worked well."

"No, it hasn't, John. I run into former Smith School students around town from time to time and they have that hollow look in their eyes. And after talking to them, I know why. They've taken a wrong path along their life's journey way too early, and now they're trying to get back on the right road. But it's so hard to catch up when you've got bills to pay, and a family to feed."

"I ran into the boy of a friend of mine last week at the grocery store, Brad, and he was just as you described. He basically told me he'd give anything to go back and go on to college as his parents wanted him to. He hates his job, and he has no idea what he wants to do with the rest of his life."

"Sounds like my cousin. He had so much potential, but just seemed to never know what to do with it. . . . John, on a day when you're feeling well, if your doctor says it's OK, will you come over to school and talk to the seniors about what we've been discussing here? I think I'll talk to Millie about me helping her start this new focus on senior transitions. I could assist with a guest speaker component that exposes our high schoolers to someone from the community every week who has had a vision, chased their dreams, and stayed the course."

"Will be glad to speak to the kids, Brad. . . . Now, reach me my camera. I have some photos to shoot here in this paradise you've brought me to this morning."

In The 5 Patterns of Extraordinary Careers, *James M. Citrin and Richard A. Smith (2003) detail compelling strategies for fulfilling one's vocational needs with variety and meaning. The authors stress that strengths, passion, and people are keys to work being a joy, not a burden.*

SUMMARY

Brad takes John on a nature hike, and the two discuss the need for more high school students to be supported and guided in knowing how to chart a vision for their lives. John helps Brad realize that Smith School could be more purposeful and focused in this area, and Brad invites John to visit the school to talk to seniors.

REFLECTIONS

1. What is your school's comprehensive plan, other than academic courses, for preparing students for a fulfilling life after high school?
2. How many adults are actively involved in coordinating or supporting this plan?
3. How does your school utilize volunteer mentors and/or guest speakers from the community?

Chapter Five

Principal with an Attitude

The leader assumed his followers would jump at his bark, as he bossed them to greatness. One day he looked around, and the organization was far from great, and there were no followers at all.

Life lesson: Attempting to lead when your heart is not with your people is a futile exercise of self-deception.

John looked forward to Brad's visits, and the October winds brought a sadness as he missed his mentoring work with principals. He had stayed in bed this morning, but when he heard Brad's knock at the door, he jumped up and moved to his chair in the TV room.

"There's my boy! How's everything going this week, Brad?"

"Good, very good, John. The kids are looking forward to your visit. And the faculty is, too. They like our plan to be more aggressive in helping our seniors to take their next steps wisely as they prepare to leave Smith School. Actually, the issue that's causing me some concerns presently is in regard to one of the principals I'm mentoring in your program."

"Is he overwhelmed?"

"Hardly. More like overinflated ego and out of touch with reality."

"How long has he been a principal?"

"This is his second year, and he seems to think he learned all there is to know about leadership in year one. But in reality, he doesn't know what he doesn't know. From what I'm picking up on already, in terms of relationships, he doesn't even have a clue."

"Happens all the time, Brad. I continue to be amazed at how many very talented people who are placed in leadership positions miss the mark in the area of human resources. I'm afraid this is something we're not spending near enough time on in our prep programs. The people factor—emotional intelligence and all that goes with it, is not just a key piece; it is *the most important piece* of effective leadership."

"Well, this guy sure doesn't have it, John. He's like a bull in a china shop."

"Brad, from his perspective, what's going on? Is he distracted with too much other stuff in his life? Is he not developing other leaders and then delegating work throughout the organization? Does he not see himself as others are seeing him?"

"He's weak in all three of these areas, John. For a principal in only his second year, he seems to have after-school responsibilities outside of his school work that never end. I wonder if he's ever home with his family. He seems to be very interested in climbing the social ladder, and is already talking of being a superintendent some day. Thus, this preoccupation with goals other than his school leads to his making too many impulsive decisions to save time."

Brad raised his voice, obviously agitated. "Empowering and equipping his staff and then delegating would be a wise move of course, but he doesn't even take the time to get to know his staff. It's as if he approaches his school as a factory, and his staff as his assembly-line workers. And no, he has no idea how guarded his staff trust is toward him. He gives out no authentic empathy or compassion, and thus, there's not any in return."

"Is he coming to your principals' small group?"

"Doesn't seem to think he needs it. And oh how he would benefit from that support network of colleagues! These are the types of real issues we talk about."

"What about the kids, Brad? Does he connect with the students?"

"No. Doesn't know many names, doesn't show them a lighter side up close and personal—not even in assemblies."

"Brad, what's the worst thing you've seen him do this fall thus far? Obviously he's managing the school instead of leading it—but that can work for a while. Perhaps he's very, very salvageable."

"The worst thing I've seen him do? Let me list three that immediately come to mind. He fired a custodian the first week of school this fall because an influential parent complained about a smelly bathroom. Strictly a political move to look strong in the face of adversity. When I asked him later if he had a list of documented complaints on this employee, he said he didn't have time to write stuff down. A veteran teacher told me later that the staff was embarrassed about this, because this custodian had been doing a good job for the year he had worked there."

"The second issue I witnessed that shocked me was his dressing down of a new teacher in front of her colleagues in a teachers' meeting. She had forgotten an early-morning bus duty. Again, this was a grandstanding ploy to force respect from the staff. This teacher did not have a history of being late, nor had he even talked to her much about anything the first few days of school—even though she was brand new and needed a lot of support and guidance."

"What's the third example?"

"I've seen him tell his secretary to make some numbers work so her recordkeeping on a couple of grants would be in line with what the district office expected. Certainly left room for interpreting that he was giving her permission to fudge ethically, and the expression on her face showed me that she was very uncomfortable with this approach to fiscal management."

"Have you had the core value talk with him yet, Brad?"

"No, but I realize it's time."

"Would you like for me to sit in on that conversation with you?"

"That would be awesome, John. What if I arranged to have him accompany me to a session here at your home next week?"

"Let's do it."

"I'll be honest with you, John. He may get pretty obstinate with you."

"Brad, I am very ill with cancer. This man sounds like he's an embarrassment to our profession, with plans of moving right on through the bureaucracy until he lands a job as the CEO of an entire district. I think we can help him. I know he has to change or his staff, the students, and the entire community will suffer until the day he leaves that school. I don't really care if he gets upset at me. That's been the cowardly attitude that's taken precedent much too long in education. I'll just simply help him understand that he's at a crossroads in his career, whether he realizes it or not. Is he in or out? That's what he needs to ask himself in the mirror and then decide if he truly wants to listen, learn, and change."

"See you next week, John. May I bring a second car, in case I need a ride home?"

John threw his head back and laughed loudly. "No, I'll call you a taxi if you're stranded here after our little pow wow."

In Failing Forward, *John C. Maxwell (2000) embraces failure as a stepping stone to learning life lessons that lead to needed change and effectiveness.*

SUMMARY

Brad seeks John's counsel on how to effectively mentor a principal who is out of touch with the impact his weak leadership is having on the people in his school, seemingly distracted with his goal to move on up the political ladder. John agrees to intervene.

REFLECTIONS

1. Have you ever worked under a leader who was out of touch with the needs of the organization?
2. What did the staff do to cope with this disconnect?
3. Would a culture of honest debate and transparent conversation have helped this person to see the leadership gaps that others were seeing?

Chapter Six

Intervention

Sometimes, what breaks the spell of denial is for someone to simply care enough to look you square in the eye and say: "You're hurting people."

Life lesson: The teaching profession is less respected than it should be largely due to the minority of discontents who do not have "the right stuff" to genuinely care for kids every day.

As Brad turned into John's driveway, he thought to himself: "Would I have the courage to do what John is doing for me today for one of my colleagues? He is standing in the gap for me big time on this one."

"Hello, Brad. Glad you guys could make it. I've got some donuts and juice in here for you all. Let's go into the kitchen and do some snacking while we chat."

"Thanks, John. We'll take you up on that. Are the donuts cream-filled?"

"Sure are."

"Oh my, how can we resist? . . . John, this is Nathan Adams. He's one of the principals I'm working with this year in your program, and I wanted him to meet you."

"Welcome, Nathan. So good for you to come. Yes, Brad told me you'd be tagging along this morning. We have found in our work with principals that the one-to-one and small-group talk time is critical. You folks don't get to do that with anyone at school, and thus can be left alone on an island day after day with no lifeline, or so it may feel that way." John reached out his hand to greet Nathan.

Nathan seemed so agitated by John's comment that he forgot to return the handshake. "Actually, sir, I don't feel that way at all. I've never felt like I was in over my head, or needed extra counseling from another principal. But, my superintendent insisted I take part in this program with Brad this year, so here I am."

John's smile left his face. "Your superintendent's a wise man. Usually, the leader is the last to know when he or she's in over their head."

Brad cleared his throat and went ahead into the kitchen, thinking to himself, "Oh boy, here we go."

"In over my head, sir?" Nathan's face turned red.

"Come on in, Nathan. Grab a chair and a donut." John walked slowly behind the two younger men, not wanting to reveal that he had had a rough week with his chemotherapy. As he sat down and reached for his glass of orange juice that he had already been drinking earlier that morning, he scooted closer to Nathan and asked, "Talk to me about your core values."

"Core values?"

"Yep. Deep down inside Nathan, tell me what you're about."

Nathan shifted in his chair, nervously poured his own glass of juice, and began. "Well, I like boats. Big boats. I plan to retire early as soon as I get my minimum years in, and join my brother in selling boats at the marina near the state park back home where my folks live."

John smiled, and made sure Nathan felt more at ease. "I love the outdoors, too. We'll have to spend a day on the lake later this year. . . . What else?"

"I like houses. Hoping to build a new home next summer."

"What else?"

"Well, obviously, I care for my family, and my job—you know, those things are a given."

"Are they Nathan?"

"What are you getting at, sir?"

"Are family and our job a given? Do they just sort of always work out . . . always fall into place for us, while we focus our energies on these other life goals?"

"I'm not sure I follow you, sir."

"Notice, Nathan, in your reply to my question, that you mentioned a boat and a home first. Let me ask you something . . . who would be helping you buy that boat? And who would be living in that new home?"

"Well, the school district, I guess, will keep giving me a good salary so I can enjoy the finer things of life. That's one of the main reasons I went into school administration—I wasn't going to be able to make it on a teacher's salary. And to answer the second part, obviously, my wife and kids would live in the home with me."

"But what if the boat and the new home weren't options, Nathan? Who would still be there helping take care of you, loving you, and needing you every day?"

"Well, my family, of course."

"And what if the higher-paying principal's job had not come along?"

"Well I guess I'd have found a job somewhere else, or I'd still be stuck in the classroom."

"Stuck in the classroom?"

"Well, you know what I mean."

"Who would be surrounding you every day at work with their smiles, and personalities, and whims, and idiosyncrasies?"

"Kids."

"Nathan, this is the first time you've mentioned students. Why do you think that is?"

"Well, I thought you obviously knew that if I was an educator, kids would be in the equation."

"But I guess I'm a little surprised that you mentioned a boat and a new home first, instead of your wife, your own children, and the students who looked to you for guidance and mentoring every day as a teacher, and now look to you to be an awesome role model as a principal."

"John, if it's OK to call you by your first name, I just don't think your point makes sense. Just because I have goals that go beyond home and school, that doesn't mean I don't care for the people in my life."

"No, maybe not, Nathan. But it speaks volumes about your priorities . . . where your mind is . . . where your heart is. Let me ask you another question. How did your students like you when you were in the classroom?"

"Never thought much about it. I taught the ol' fashioned way. I had rules; I had procedures; I had daily and weekly work they had to do. If they fell in line, everything was fine. If they bucked my system, they didn't do so well in my classroom."

"And how did the parents respond to that style of classroom management?"

"To be honest, John, I didn't care too much about what the parents thought either. It was my job to run the classroom. It was their job to teach their children to respect me, obey me, and get with the program. Those who figured that out seemed to make it through the year just fine."

"Were there a lot of requests each summer for students to be in your room?"

"Never asked, never cared."

"Did you ever do a parent survey to find out what they felt about your skills as a teacher?"

"Nope."

"Ever do a survey with your students?"

"Nope. Didn't need little kids telling me, an adult, how to teach."

"Did you ever seek input from your fellow teachers?"

"Sure. We all vented and shared ideas in the teacher's lounge at lunch. That was our chance to set the record straight on just how ridiculous some parts of the schooling business are."

"Any of your colleagues ever offer to help you with your classroom dynamics?"

"I can't remember. But I sure wouldn't have appreciated it. I knew what I was doing."

"Did your principal ever point out areas of your work that needed more development—in his conversations with you, or on your growth plan, or end-of-year evaluation?"

"Nope. He was pretty much like me. He felt that grown men and women with college degrees could surely manage a school full of children."

"And is this your philosophy on leading a school as the principal? Basically, you're managing it, and folks should chill out and just do their job."

"Yes, that pretty much defines it, John. Listen, I see where you're going with all of this, and I deeply resent it. I know how to run a classroom, and I know how to run a school."

"But do you know anything about teaching as a caring mentor to a precious little child who wants to think you hung the moon? And do you know anything about leading a school of teachers and staff who so hope you are the real deal, someone they can believe in, and trust, and look up to?"

"Sounds like you're asking me to be a Pollyanna, John—you know, a do-gooder who wants *everybody* to be happy. If I did that, my teachers would run all over me."

"Would they, Nathan? I'm going to ask you to do one simple task for me, and then I'm going to ask you to come back in a few days and share with me the results. If you don't want to be in our mentoring program after that, it's fine with me if you drop out, and I'm sure Brad would be glad to release you so he could add someone who really wanted to learn some things about school leadership."

"Fair enough. What's the task? I'll do it tomorrow if I can. I would love to be excused from this program."

"I want you to gather all your staff in the library one day after school this coming week, and ask them these three questions. If you have a notepad, please write them down."

"Ok. I'm ready—fire away."

"First question: 'What does my principal do well in serving this school?'

"Next, 'What would I like to see my principal do more of in serving this school?'

"And finally, 'Does my principal care for our staff and our students in a way that models compassion and heart-to-heart relationship?'"

"What type of a survey is that, John? Sounds like a character ed lesson at Boy Scout camp."

"You ever go to Boy Scout camp, Nathan?"

"Well, no. My summers were always too busy."

"Out on your Dad's boat, or home in your Mom's house, right?"

"Yeah, pretty much."

"Thanks for dropping by, Nathan. I look forward to visiting with you again next week. Bring the survey results with you." Brad didn't say a word, but simply ushered Nathan to the door. John winced in pain and slowly made his way back to bed.

In Moral Intelligence, *Doug Lennick and Fred Kiel (2008) illustrate the huge gaps that exist in any individual or organizational leadership model when integrity and character are not front and center.*

SUMMARY

Brad brings his self-focused principal colleague to John's house for a chat. John lays it all on the line, challenging the young administrator to take a good look at his priorities, and asks him to simply survey his staff about his leadership skills.

REFLECTIONS

1. Can an uncaring, overwhelmed, or distracted administrator be cured of his (or her) leadership gaps? If so, how?
2. Does your school conduct regular staff self-assessments that allow for ongoing work on individual professional growth?
3. Would you feel the freedom in your school to provide candid feedback to your principal, or other colleagues? To receive it as well?

Chapter Seven

The Man in the Mirror

I lived in an illusion of wellness, somehow pretending that I was the man I dreamed I could be. One day, someone loved me enough to tell me the truth, and I stepped out of the fog long enough to see what I had really become. From that day on, I began my journey to true significance in the lives of others. It has been a long road, but now I am giving more than taking—and I have a peace I never had before.

Life lesson: Caring for someone enough to help them face their dysfunctions is a love of the deepest kind.

Brad was on a trip to the state department to report on the progress of the principal mentoring program, and Nathan was relieved. He felt he needed to visit John alone this time. When he pulled into the driveway, he noticed that John's wife, Marge, was sitting in her car. As Nathan walked by and started to wave, he saw that Marge was crying.

Nathan pecked on the window, and offered that maybe he should come back another day. "Are you Nathan?" Marge wiped away her tears the best she could.

"Yes, ma'am."

"No, you go on in, Nathan. He's been hoping you'd make it this morning, and told me this was the most important thing he would do all week. You must be very special."

Nathan lowered his head, and said in a low voice, "I don't think so."

"Come in, come in, Nathan. I am so glad you called yesterday. You kept your word, and I appreciate it more than you know. Let's go into the living room, so I can sit in my chair. . . . May I get you something to eat?"

"No, sir, but thank you. Actually, I had breakfast over at school this morning. First time I'd even been in there with the kids, and it felt good."

"Did this new priority come out of your staff survey?"

"Yes, sir, I guess it did."

"Well, what do you think? Were your staff fair with you?"

"Yes, sir, I think they were . . . and before we go any further, I just want to apologize to you for being so rude last week when you were just being genuine with me, and taking time to care. You were real, you were honest, and you weren't afraid to confront my attitude and my blind spots. And I am eternally grateful."

"So you're seeing some things through a different lens?"

"If you only knew, sir. I was so hot when I left here last week, I couldn't wait to get home and get my wife to tell me what a bully you were, and how off base your assessment of my core values and priorities were. But, she did not. Instead, we had the best talk we've had since before we got married. It went on for about three hours. We cried, we laughed, we hugged, and most important—I listened. For the first time, I stopped assuming and rationalizing, and instead found the courage to ask my wife how I am really doing as a husband and a father."

"How are you doing, Nathan?"

"Oh, about a two on a scale of ten. We've decided to go to a marriage counselor so we can keep these conversations going. I am just amazed, John, at how out of touch I had become. Talk about an illusion. . . . I had become a world-class jerk, and was pretending to myself that everything was fine."

"I am so proud of you Nathan. . . . So, how did the staff survey go?"

Nathan stopped talking, and just stared out the window for several seconds, with tears in his eyes. Finally, he cleared his throat and spoke with a trembling voice.

"My staff could not believe I would ask them to give me such honest feedback. I could see a couple actually sniffling and wiping their eyes as they wrote. The library got so quiet, you could have heard a pin drop. Some stayed for about an hour, John, just writing and writing."

"What were some of their comments, if you don't mind sharing?"

"Oh, I don't mind at all. This is part of the cleansing that I need to be going through if I have any chance of getting my life together, John. Little did I know, but not only was I in danger of losing my family, but I was in danger of losing my career. The staff had actually met a week earlier, and were going to go to the superintendent at the end of the semester and ask him if he could move me somewhere else. They couldn't stand it anymore."

"What do you think they couldn't stand?"

"Me not being there for them and their students."

"Anything else?"

"Well, they gave lots of examples, but that's it in a nutshell. One person said she was pretty sure I still didn't know her name. Another shared that her father had died, and I had not even acknowledged it, much less made it to the funeral."

"Had you known about it, Nathan?"

"No. . . . Oh, I might remember vaguely someone at school telling me about it, but it didn't register. . . . I was so ashamed when I realized I'd not offered her any comfort. Not any at all."

"So they weren't so much thirsting for your being a wizard with technology, or curriculum, or in writing grants, as they were in dire need of your compassion and supporting them as people who you believe in, and want to help any way you can."

"Exactly, John. I was running that school like I mow my grass. . . . Just do it when it needs it, get it over with—with my mind wandering off in all directions. After all, it's just grass. Somehow, I was treating that school and its people the same way. . . . 'It's just a school. Let's get the job done every day and go home.' . . . No wonder I didn't know everyone's name. I was treating them like objects, John."

"And I bet the students and their parents were sensing this disconnect, too."

"Oh my, yes! As a matter of fact, several staff commented on their surveys that they could handle my indifference if I would only pay attention to the kids, and be some type of a positive role model for them."

"Well, I guess my next question is, what has changed in your school since you and your staff had this very transparent meeting that laid so much right out there on the table?"

"We are alive again. . . . I had let the entire school community slowly but surely die. But, now there are signs of being reborn. And, it basically begins and ends with me. As goes my attitude, so goes the school. I realize that now—never had admitted this to myself before. So, I'm starting the day by recognizing students and staff on the intercom during morning announcements for special things they have accomplished, including birthdays, anniversaries, science projects, art contest winners . . . whatever the accolades can include that day. And, I'm mingling with the kids. I am amazed at how much they like this. I just never thought it mattered."

"Are the staff letting you know they can tell a difference in the school culture?"

"Yes, they are thrilled. I am meeting with them one to one and in small groups in their team meetings, and just listening, taking notes, asking them how they need me to support. It's absolutely amazing, John. All they've ever wanted from me was for me to care. And, sadly, until this week, I guess I never did."

"You have made the most important decision you may ever make in your entire life, Nathan. You've chosen the servant leadership model. I promise you, you'll never regret it. You'll never look back. And, now, the sky's the limit in terms of how happy and fulfilled you can be, and how happy and fulfilled you can make others—at home, and out there in the world."

"I know, John. I know. It's as if I've been given a second chance to truly be who I am capable of being. For all intents and purposes, I had relegated myself to the junk heap, although I was living in such self-delusion I certainly didn't see it that way."

"Well I can tell you one thing, Nathan—Brad is going to be thrilled. He has been very concerned about you. Will you join his principals' cadre? I think you'd love the flavor and support of that group."

"I'd love to. And, I need it, John."

As Nathan got up to leave, he turned and gave John a hug. "Thank you, sir, for caring for a self-centered jerk like me."

John smiled, shook Nathan's hand firmly, and said, "I'll see you later. I want us to talk again."

As Nathan drove out of the driveway, Marge hurried in and helped John get ready for his doctor's visit. He had a treatment scheduled, and he was running late. But, he didn't care. He smiled and thought to himself, "Nathan was more important than that ol' treatment. I am so glad I was here for him today."

In If You Don't Feed the Teachers They Eat the Students! *Neila A. Conners (2000) offers an array of examples of why it is so helpful to a school's culture if the administrator(s) will take the extra time to let teachers know their work is appreciated.*

SUMMARY

Nathan keeps his promise, and surveys his staff about his qualities and tendencies as a leader. But, he first has a heart-to-heart discussion with his wife. When he visits John again, he is a changed man.

REFLECTIONS

1. Does your staff and members of your school's administrative team have opportunities to participate in one-to-one and cohort mentoring programs?

2. How are we conditioned by the status quo to minimize the importance of building strong relationships among staff and with students?
3. Name some new ways that students and staff in your school could be recognized for their various accomplishments and successes.

Chapter Eight

A Preferable Future

The master walked down the wooded trail, thinking back with each step on how he could have made a bigger impact during his journey. And he walked faster, realizing his gift now was to his pupils, as he passed the torch to the next generation.

Life lesson: Spending time with someone who has lived a life of integrity and commitment to others is time well spent indeed—and can change one's perspective in life-changing ways.

Brad picked John up at his home early on the Monday before Thanksgiving, so excited that John was going to join the principals' cadre that was meeting at Smith School later that morning.

"How have they been responding to your sessions, Brad?" John talked slowly, and with a lower voice than usual. Brad could tell that the chemotherapy had taken its toll. But, his prayer was that it was also killing out John's cancer.

"John, I can't be you. So, to say the group's discussions have been as rich as last year, I'm not going to kid here—we've missed you. But, on the other hand, each month our meetings have been helpful, and the group keeps growing. I'm so glad it was Smith School's turn to host. Millie has had a meal prepared for the group that is going to be divine. And, she can't wait to share with you how she's doing, too. Her visit with you was so, so helpful."

"Did she get her assistant principal?"

"Sure did. When Dr. Cobb realized how much we'd changed the formula from last year—with me taking over your role for a while, and being gone so much—he gave Millie some help within the week. I am amazed at how serious he is about meeting the needs of his people down in the trenches."

"That's why he's such a great superintendent, Brad. He's not gotten above his raising. He truly listens to and cares for his staff in his schools. He realizes that's the key to the kids being given the best education possible."

As John got out of the car, he had to use a cane. Some of the principals he had worked with the year before rushed out from the front door of the school to help him inside. Some had to turn away to wipe away tears from their eyes.

But John had a big smile on his face as he sat down around the table in the corner of the lunchroom. For there, sitting with him, were not only Brad and Millie, but also Linda and Todd, and others whom he had mentored over the last three years.

"Hello, everybody." John took off his hat and sat back with a peacefulness that can only be felt by someone who has lived a good life. His hair was gone, and as he realized what he had done, he smiled and put the hat right back on.

"How do you want to do this, John?" Brad wanted this meeting to be special, and for the group to gain as much from John's wisdom as possible. Oh how he wished, at this moment, that he was still serving Smith School, and John was running the mentoring program.

"Let's just keep taking questions, Brad. I've got all day." John looked around the table at this fine group of young leaders who he had spent hours and hours with in providing support and guidance. He had missed them so.

"I'll start." Linda held a handkerchief in her hand, and tried not to let her voice break. Two years earlier, she had been John's first candidate in the mentoring program, and was now already recognized as one of the best young principals in the state. "John, what's it feel like to be home, away from the stress of leading a school? I find myself thinking sometimes that I'm giving my all to my school, when perhaps I should slow down and re-think my career goals at this stage."

"What do you enjoy most, Linda?"

"Helping people . . . especially children."

"Do you still get excited when a new school year begins?"

"Yes, I sure do. As the principal, I still get those butterflies the night before opening day, and still love going with my own kids for school supplies. And when all the staff start coming back in off summer break, I can't wait to see them. And on that first morning, when the buses roll in, I love to see the students again, how they've grown over the summer, and how they smile and say 'hello' to me."

"Sounds like you love this work, Linda. When it's time to do something different, you'll know. And that doesn't mean you have to retire, even then. Look at me—I was blessed to get to serve as a mentor to wonderful folks like you all sitting around this table. And I'd give anything to be out there this year, too—visiting schools, discussing leadership with principals, meeting with small groups like this."

John looked off in the distance. "Shifting gears is not so much about retiring—that's a myth. It's about making adjustments in our work at various stages of our career perhaps. But, as my dad used to always say: 'Do we ever really retire?' As long as there are people who need us, we have lots of important and fulfilling work to do. Your school needs you, Linda. Sounds like you still have the fire down inside. Keep making a difference. Keep loving on people."

The group sat still, realizing that John was sick, very sick . . . but still wanting so much to give back to those who needed him. His passion for his work moved each one of them. His love of life, and of people, reminded them all why they got up before daylight and came to work every day.

Todd held up his hand, and cleared his throat. "John, what would you do, if you were me? I am the principal of a high school that just keeps growing and growing, and getting better and better. Sometimes, to be honest, I feel like I need two of me to keep up with the pace."

"Let go."

"Let go? Just how do I do that?"

"Are you still taking your family on those quarterly get-a-ways, Todd?"

"Sure am. And I owe you for that, John. Best thing I ever did in terms of what was best for my family."

"Never thought you'd find time to do that every three months, did you—until you just finally one fall started making the time. And I bet Todd, all the little things on your 'to do' list don't seem to matter when it comes to those trips with your family. It's amazing how it works: what needs to truly get done, gets done. It's the same way with leading a school. Keep the priorities where they should be: mingle with your people, spend a lot of time with the kids, empower and equip your staff and other human resources, and it will all fall into place—no matter how big the job seems to be at times."

"You make it sound so easy, John. Give me an example. What should I let go of right now? I mean, the school's doing awesome, so it's not like we're in a downward spiral. But, if you were me, what would you let go?"

"What consumes your time, Todd, that you would rather not have to deal with every day at this point of your career?"

"Meetings at central office, regional events I'm supposed to go to, lots of ballgames that make my days so, so long."

"How many assistant principals do you have?"

"Two."

"I'd keep giving these opportunities to learn more about your job to them, 'cause most likely they'll be doing it some day. And, I'd make sure, whatever it takes, that you re-arrange your weekly schedule so you're not out night after night with school responsibilities. This one thing wears out more principals, especially middle and high school, than anything else. . . . How many staff do you have, Todd?"

"Altogether, we have about sixty, counting part-time."

"And you have an athletic director, and about ten coaches, right?"

"That's about right."

"You'll figure it out. Put some of those less important meetings, and some of those evening activities on your 'not to do' list, and spend some time looking at all the human resources you have access to. I bet by next week, you'll have come up with a plan that will take much of this stuff off of your shoulders."

"Is it really that easy, John? I mean, I'm needed at all of these meetings, and games."

"That's where you're wrong Todd. You *think* you are supposed to be working fifteen-hour days, and that time at school makes you a great principal. Actually, it doesn't. What makes you a great principal is how much you care for your school, and then how you help others to take on responsibility in helping you share that servant leadership. You've been there for a few years now. It's time you decreased, so others can increase."

"So, letting go is not a selfish thing, but actually, an unselfish way of coordinating so we keep adding capacity—not slowly drowning one by one as we can't keep up the pace."

"You got it, Todd. Remember, as the principal, you're the conductor of the orchestra. There's a whole lot of members who can play a whole lot of instruments very well. You certainly can't play those instruments for them. But, you can silently lead the group to doing things collectively that they would have never done, or you would have never done, on your own."

"'Not to do' list. . . . I like that, John." Todd smiled and made some notes.

Millie spoke up. "John, if you could only tell us one thing that you would do in growing a great school, what would it be?"

"Love on people. Real and authentic relationships with students. Same thing with staff. Same thing with parents. Same thing with the community. I have a cousin who is one of the best pastors I've ever known. I visited his church last summer while on vacation and asked him what his secret was. He simply said, 'I love them, John. I spend a lot of time in their homes getting to know them on a personal, deeper level; I visit them in the hospitals when they are sick; and I cast a vision every Sunday morning about what their lives could be if they will but believe. That's really all I do. I'm not very good at administration and all the paperwork. But, I do love people. So, that's where I focus my energy. . . . I just keep loving them.'"

Millie smiled. "The answer's right there in front of us, isn't it?"

"It always is, Millie. It always is."

Brad shook his head from side to side in disgust, and seemed to not want to say what he blurted out. "John, no matter how hard I try, I seem to always have a teacher or two, and a parent or two, who make life miserable for the rest of us. To be honest, I hate to see them coming. And, it never fails, they always want to unload on me with how frustrated they are over this or that."

"Do you really want to help the restless ones, Brad? The *troublemakers*, as we sometimes call them . . . the irregular people?"

"Yes, I think I really do, John."

"Then the next time they come running to you with a problem or complaint that to you probably seems so trivial, or out of sync with the rest of the school, I want you to do one thing."

"Tell me what it is, John, and I'll do it. Anything to get them to stop the endless negative talk."

"Look into their eyes, and see that little girl or little boy that they used to be. In so many ways, that's who they still are. Just like you're still a boy in many ways. Then, just listen, laugh with them, cry with them, agree with them when you can, but also tell them the truth—because they need to hear it. Connect with them, Brad. Love them enough to respect them as being just as special to your school as your strongest teachers and parents who agree with everything you say."

Brad looked toward the other end of the cafeteria. "I have definitely not been doing that. . . . You're saying, John, if I hear you correctly, to build close, authentic relationship with those who are the most unlikable?"

"Yes, Brad, that's exactly what I'm saying. You do that, and you will never see them as problems again. And, ironically, they will not bring as many complaints to you as time goes on. You give them the same respect you give your more likable folks, and they'll try very hard to not let you down."

And the questions just kept coming, as the group thirsted for more in this healing conversation with their mentor. But, John soon grew tired. As he stood up to leave, and reached for his cane, he turned to the group with a gleam in his eye and simply added, "The kids need everyone on your staff to be good to them, and to care for them. Hire that type of people, and train the rest to be that way; then model it for them every day, and you will always have great schools. For school, my dear friends, is about relationship. The mentor and the pupil—learning and growing together."

In Halftime, *Buford (1994) defines the difference between success and significance, and encourages anyone who is struggling with what is truly important in life to look inside to their core beliefs and then to live not with dread, but with passion.*

SUMMARY

Brad brings John to a principals' cohort meeting, and the group welcomes the opportunity to ask him the tougher questions about school leadership. And, to no one's surprise, he doesn't let them down.

REFLECTIONS

1. Do you belong to a professional learning community that meets regularly to discuss the real issues of your work?
2. Does your school district encourage the creating of "think tank" and support groups throughout the organization?
3. Does your principal belong to a support group such as the one described in this chapter?

Chapter Nine

When I Was Young . . .

When I was young, I thought old age was so far away. It snuck up on me . . .
way, way too soon.

Life lesson: Those who burn the midnight oil in living a life of service to
others need times of respite along the way—regular periods of "rest and
renewal" so they can finish strong.

Brad's fall sessions with John had had a profound impact on him, and he
wanted to do something quite different this December as Christmas was fast
approaching. But, he wanted to get John's advice first. He was thrilled when
Marge said John would feel like going out for breakfast.

"Well, ol' boy, thank you for getting me out of the house again." John
chuckled as he buckled his seat belt and looked forward to something that
had become very, very special—a meal without the fear of not being able to
keep it down.

"Yeah, Marge told me the new medicine is working like a charm. That's
great news, John."

"Well, it sure is less nauseating—let's put it that way. Whether it's
working long term, we'll see I guess. Main thing, Brad, I'm praying about it,
and not worrying about it . . . very little of it in my control anyway at this
point. But I sure can tell you, I don't take anything for granted anymore.
Every day has so, so much magic in it. If we could only realize this when
we're young, oh what different lives people would live!"

Brad nodded in agreement. "That's what I wanted to talk to you about this morning, John. You see, after your visit with the cadre last week, I got to thinking about what you were trying to get across to the group. It really is about the eternal principles of goodness, isn't it? Everything else revolves around those basic rules of how to truly live life right."

"Yes, Brad. All that really ends up being important to us over the long haul is our relationships with other people. Take away the others in our lives, and really, what have we been working for all these years? A house? Expensive cars? A large bank account? A retirement plan? None of that stuff matters at the end of the game."

"So, John, for this Christmas, I want to do something really special for the principals I'm working with, and something really special to help Millie and all the folks down at Smith School. But, this is always such a hectic time of year for schools. I've been racking my brain, and I can't think of how to pull it off."

"What if you gave them a day off, but added one request—that they would spend it with their families in a very special way, and then come back refreshed with a great idea to do what you are talking about for their own schools?"

"You mean, like a one-day *sabbatical*?"

"That's exactly what I mean. Don't know why we don't do it more often in school work. Colleges and universities figured out a long time ago that their professors would benefit greatly by every few years being given several months to rest and renew. Then, they come back with a new gleam in their eye—with fresh ideas for research, for writing, and for teaching."

"Makes way too much sense, John. Who would go for such a thing?"

"Oh, I bet Dr. Cobb would buy into this concept big time, if he knew Millie and his other principals would utilize this time wisely. I wouldn't mind at all to call him and start the discussion. But, what I would need you to do is to be ready to go to the principals' cadre and give them some first-year suggestions so they can indeed pull this off, enjoy it, and prove that it can make such a difference for them, and for their schools."

"Oh my, John, I'm thinking right now, if I had a free day like this that just popped up on the calendar, I'd take my wife to a resort up in the mountains, and I'd leave all e-mails, all office work, all phone calls, and my calendar at home. I'd do it tomorrow if I could."

"And if you were a principal, then how would you come back and give a similar gift to your staff?"

"Well, perhaps in year one, I'd figure out a way to bring in subs so our five most senior staff could have a day away—free to go on a one-day sabbatical. Perhaps even, we'd make it two days for our veterans, but also one day for all staff by using volunteers from the community to come in and help with activities with the kids on those days. Perhaps I as the principal and my assistants would help work with the kids on these days. Perhaps we'd schedule a half-day assembly, and bring in some real nice cultural artists, or do our talent show on that day."

Brad's voice peaked as the wheels were turning. "When you think about it, we do this some anyway, but it's packaged differently from school to school. Yet we don't do it in a way that lets the staff know that they are so deeply appreciated, we want to honor them by giving them a holiday before the holiday, so to speak."

"And I bet, Brad, if your principals would think this through, and do this in a very organized way that did not take away from the end of the fall semester, but actually added to the culture of the school and the students' learning opportunities during the Christmas season, it would only be the starting point of something long term that became a key part of the school's annual calendar."

"And, John, wouldn't it be so wonderful if we could indeed let this be the seed that got us thinking more about sabbaticals for educators in the P–12 world?"

"Well, I will just say this. Some of these colleagues of ours who have retired early, or are so burned out and run down they can't see much to look forward to for the next several years, would certainly benefit from having a block of time—even if just a few weeks—built into one of their semesters every few years for them to get away, go observe other schools, reflect on their profession and teaching skills. . . . I can think of two or three of my own teachers, when I was a principal, that would have greatly benefited from the school district simply giving them the blessing of time off, honored for the great work they had been doing for years for the children in our community."

"And I have a couple of principals in the cadre right now John, who so desperately need this. Not just for how much they deserve it, but for their personal health and well being."

"Then, you talk to the group, and I'll talk to Dr. Cobb, and let's see what we can do, Brad. Might be a small start here initially, but I guarantee you every principal, every teacher, every school community will benefit from this in a big way."

"How do you think all of this stuff up, John?"

"Cause I've been to the brink, Brad."

"Been to the brink?"

"I've been to the bank of the river that looks to the other side, and I realize I might be making that great crossing soon. And when you are so close to saying goodbye here, you just see things more clearly. Everything is through a new lens."

Brad's voice broke. "Don't talk that way, John."

"What way, Brad? I'm not gloomy. I'm not sad. I'm just facing reality. I do believe that I might get better. I do have faith. But I'm also accepting the odds that are against me. Too often in life, we don't face the reality, Brad, until it's too late."

"What other realities are you seeing, John, with this new lens you see through?"

"I see way too many young folks in their prime years of life running around like chickens with their heads cut off. Too little time, too many things going on all at once. . . . They wake up one day and their kids are grown, their spouse is depressed and lonely, and they look at the *toys* they've worshiped—the privileged style of living that so easily traps us into thinking we're going to live forever and that tomorrow we'll slow down for the important things. The important things are always, *always* today."

"Is this why you push on principals to take a closer look at their schools, John, and to make some changes?"

"Yes, Brad, it is. School should be a marketplace of ideas . . . a world of discovery that is a great place to work, and a great place for kids to explore and learn. But, too often, I hear school leaders, teachers, students, and parents crying out for something better. They seem to not know what school is supposed to be anymore—what it can be."

"And what can it be, John? We're all in the trenches every day doing our level best to make it work."

"And that's the problem, Brad. Hear what you just said—'make it work'? That sounds like the roughest job in the world. Sounds like a boot camp or an assembly line. A learning center should not be so forced."

"I know, John. I know. And last year, at Smith School, we took that closer look, we let ourselves be free, and it was amazing how good it felt to be alive again . . . to soar, to fly . . . to be the community of learners we became. But I can't seem to keep up in getting this message across to the principals I work with. They are so entrenched in this old traditional model of school, and every time they try to climb out, they're beaten right back down."

"Who beats them down, Brad?"

"Sometimes it's state policy that seems to never end. . . . Sometimes it's the federal mandates that seem to never end. . . . Sometimes it's local—their own district office support team that seems to have forgotten what it's like in the classroom, and thus, they boss and order, and send more and more to do. After a while, the school's culture is full of gunshot—much of it from within the camp."

"Yes, I remember. . . . I have a theory that about half of the executives and consultants across our educational landscape are somehow trying to prove how much they believe in education by trying to forget that they left the classroom because they did not have it anymore. So, this is their way of giving back—they talk a model they were not able to live themselves. It's the old 'do as I say, not as I did' game. Although, to be fair—they aren't doing this on purpose."

"But, John, it's killing those of us who are now on the front lines."

"I know. And that's absolutely got to change. . . . Hey, my favorite restaurant! How'd you know, Brad?"

"Oh, Marge mentioned it this morning when you were getting your hat."

"Come on. Let's get in there and order an omelet. Then we've got some more talking to do."

In Imaginization, *Gareth Morgan (1997) shares an array of new ideas for how to take the organization past the traditional linear model to new innovation and health.*

SUMMARY

While driving to a local restaurant for breakfast, John encourages Brad to create a new tradition with his principal cadre that would honor their school staffs before the end of the fall semester. And, the two discuss how this early Christmas present could plant the seed for P–12 educators being given much-deserved sabbaticals as they navigate through their careers.

REFLECTIONS

1. Has your school district ever celebrated the good work of its staff by providing a sabbatical of some kind for the principals and teachers?
2. What other examples of recognizing and honoring staff have been practiced in your school district?
3. How could a sabbatical program be effectively implemented in a school or district?

Chapter Ten

Seeing Through the Veil

The young warrior kept coming home from the battle with wounds and scars. Then, he stopped listening to the tribal leaders who seemed to enjoy the warring and the killing fields. One day, he went beyond the front lines, to meet those souls he had been fighting all these years. They, too, could not explain why this massacre went on—this endless waste of life. And, so, they agreed: "No more."

Life lesson: Past practice does not mean current effectiveness. The wisest leaders blaze new trails in leading their followers down a better road. . . . Today's schools still have a long way to go.

Brad quickly began to enjoy his breakfast, and made sure John did not lose his train of thought. "Now where were we, John? You were about to share with me some more of your belief that the new school of the twenty-first century cannot resemble the traditional model of the past."

"Oh, some of it will resemble the past, Brad. What teachers have been doing well for decades will remain, and should remain. But where we continue to fail our children—well, that's got to change. And it won't be legislated. That's never worked very well. It will have to come from the grassroots—just like you and the Smith School community did last year."

"Because our building burned down the first week of school and we had no choice but to start over."

"Exactly. But, in reality, other schools don't have a choice either, Brad. Our society depends on the 'school of the future' getting it right . . . as never before. This is what you must keep stressing to the principals you mentor. Have them visit Smith School, and other models like it. They must get their heads above water and see the shore. Keep them swimming for the shore, Brad."

"What must change, John? You mentioned that some of what we have called 'school' has been good. But what should go? You talked to the cadre about knowing how to 'let go.' . . . What do you think needs to be 'let go' in order for the innovative, effective school of the future to be born, and to prosper?"

"Well, for starters, it's long past time to take the sign down that says: 'Free Babysitting Service—Open 7:30 to 3:30 Monday thru Friday.'"

"How do you mean?"

"Technology begs us to restructure how we schedule school, Brad. It is wonderful when it does work out that the kids can be at school, while Mom and Dad go to work. But that can no longer be the driving force of how we structure the school day, or school week. We're still thinking with an Industrial Age 9 AM to 5 PM mentality, and we've grown far beyond that era and the model that might have worked well back then. But maybe even then, it didn't. Dropout rates down through history would tell us it's never worked real well."

"But how would you do it differently, John?"

"I wouldn't do anything drastic across the board. One size fits all does not work. Transformative change is grassroots, local, in *your* community, in *your* school. I'd start by unchaining schools and districts from so many of these mandated structures. Yes, there would still be school days, and weeks, and yearly calendars. But if a school wanted to take the winter months off because the weather is so bad in their neck of the woods, they would be given that freedom. Or if a school wanted to offer an abundance of evening classes and weekend classes for kids who had good reasons to come at those hours, it would be allowed to do so.

"If a school wanted to provide much more cooperative education in the community with local businesses and even farmers, for example, there would not be endless hoops to jump through. And if a school wanted to go to a half-day online model, with at least some students having the freedom to come to school in the morning, or vice versa, then go home the other half of the day to do their work on the Internet, or be free for clubs and music or ball practice, or field trips, or college classes, or internships—those types of options would be plentiful."

"But wouldn't that upset the apple cart, John? Wouldn't that create chaos?"

"Not if the adults who raise and teach these kids really thought it through. Too often, with our current model, the school calendar is designed for the convenience of the adults in the community—much more so than for the kids."

"I used to think it was the other way around—that we cater to the kids too much."

"Picking kids up on buses before daylight, and getting them home at 5 PM, sometimes later than their parents get home from work—that's catering to the kids, Brad? . . . Is haphazardly cutting out music and band programs, art and physical education due to budget issues catering to the kids, Brad? . . . Is, across the board in our American culture, around 30 percent of high school freshmen dropping out at some point before making it to graduation day a system that caters to the kids? . . . Is a process that is so antiquated that many, many students suffer through their rigid, uninspiring schedules at school, then rush home to do their real learning on the Internet catering to the kids?"

"OK, OK, I get it, John. You're right. We have not seemed to have thought through these issues in a way that embraces the future and all the flexibility and resources we have at our fingertips. Now, you've got my attention. What other examples can you think of?"

"Poor teachers."

"Yep, as a principal, I realize now that this is an issue that should be non-negotiable. Bottom line, the common denominator in all great schools is the abundance of great teachers."

"You're exactly right, son. So then why do we still sweep this issue under the rug? Would any other profession live in such illusion? Are poor doctors given such latitude? Do bankers who can't balance the books get to keep their jobs? Do we reward CEOs who can't lead companies? Don't answer that one—poor example! . . . I'm not trying to be cruel here, Brad. I firmly believe that a weak or mediocre teacher can be coached and guided along so they do indeed develop the needed skills. But, their weaknesses need to be addressed immediately, and then after an adequate time of being developed, if they aren't master teachers, they need to be helped to another profession, or another area of education—but not in the classroom."

"In reality, John, wouldn't this one thing fix most of our problem?"

"Much of it, but not all of it."

"What other visions do you have for a bright future in the education of our children, John?"

"I see school communities being given the freedom to hold parents accountable for their child's education. Not only volunteering hours to support the school, but signing contracts that they will provide an education-rich environment at home. If the school provides a laptop for a child, that parent should be given training on how to use that laptop as well, so they can monitor the work that should be going on at home."

"And if they don't work with the school?"

"If they won't come in for regular conferences with the school team that works with their child, if they don't show evidence that they are doing their part at home, if they are not truly being a loving parent and a positive role model for their kid, then surely we can find ways to provide them with consequences. I know, Brad, that if I don't pay my property taxes on time, if

I file my income tax late, if I don't keep my driver's license current, if I don't report for jury duty when summoned, and so on, and so on, I will have to pay for my lack of maturity. In regard to the educating of our youth, and the role the home plays, surely we can provide more guidance, and help with boundaries."

"Yep, it is indeed the teacher's fault or the home's fault, when a child isn't learning at school."

"But not always, son, not always. We've heaped so much nonsense on our teachers in recent years, many of them will tell you they're so busy doing all the paperwork and bureaucratic do's and don'ts, the time left for teaching and learning with their classroom of kids has become less than ever."

"I have noticed in a couple of the schools I visit, John, with the intercom interruptions, the helter-skelter pace of the school day, and the lack of good flow, it just seems the general culture of the school is out of wack. These schools appear to be more like busy shopping malls—lots of frenzy and everyone rushing here and there. I don't know how to explain it—it just seems to be not what was intended. And the staff—from the principal to the teachers to the secretary—always just seem so stressed . . . like they don't want to even be there, but they have to be."

"It's not just in one or two schools, Brad. I have sisters and nieces and nephews who are in education, and they tell me that it's not fun to be a teacher anymore. Instead, they feel like robots—always being given more work from above to do."

"How would we change this, John? It seems to be a monster that has just kept growing for so long, now no one knows how to stop it."

"Only one way to stop it."

"How's that?"

"One school at a time. One principal going in one day and telling his teachers: 'Just be the mentor and role model for these kids you know how to be. Love on these kids, visit their homes, build relationships with their parents. Play in these classrooms some, too—stop grinding the kids so much in such boring ways that they would rather go to work at the factory with their Dad! Come alive again as mentors with your pupils. I'm turning you loose. Let this school be an open doorway to dreams coming true, an endless stream of creativity, a light in the center of the community that everyone wants to be a part of in some way.'"

"Sort of like what we did last year at Smith School."

"Yes. We must return the classroom to the teacher, Brad, and to the students. We must give them our blessing, and trust that they will know what to do. And then we must give them the resources they need . . . the extra manpower, the technology, the flexibility to do innovative projects, and field trips, and to bring in artisans and craftsmen from various fields—the empowerment to make school inspiring for everyone who walks in the door.

It's not a complicated formula. And one by one, you young leaders who are at the helm right now can do this. You must do this . . . or there will be dire consequences for our society like we have never seen."

"You mean it could get worse?"

"Get worse? Brad, we're spiraling downward. What the current model of education and other broken systems in our culture has given us is a society without a northern compass. Less and less embracing of the core values that protect the common good, more poverty and welfare, higher unemployment, various addictions that rage across our society, tremendous national debt, a growing class system of "haves" and "have nots" . . . and other toxic issues that collectively threaten to take the American dream to the very brink of extinction.

"The American schooling system can no longer live in an insulated bubble, Brad, numbed that it is helpless to do anything radically different to stop the killing fields—where the minds of our youth too often waste away. We are a huge part of the problem, and society's healing and the hope of a bright future begins right in that little classroom down the road."

"But I thought we were going to get more funding from the state and the feds to address these issues?"

"And we have been doing that for years, son. How can more funding help when the system it funds is broken? That's like giving more alcohol to an alcoholic. It's not the funding, Brad. It's the nuts and bolts of how to run a true child-centered classroom . . . a true child-centered school. It's about the most simplistic and effective of learning models—the mentor and the pupil—set free in authentic relationship to learn together."

"Sounds like it is indeed a rethinking of the very framework of how we even do school."

"Exactly. When the dam breaks, you don't rebuild it the same way. When a bridge falls, you take a real good look at how it was structurally designed. When a teaching/learning system hasn't met the human needs it should have, you don't just put band aids on the cancer, you start over. . . . Speaking of cancer, Brad, we should go. I've not been this emotional and fired up in months. So, I better get home and take a good nap. This was good though, Brad. This was good therapy indeed."

In Leadership Gold, *John C. Maxwell (2008) offers a rich resource of helpful principles and strategies that point out the advantage of any leader being coached by a master mentor.*

SUMMARY

Brad seeks John's vision for what the school of the future might look like, and John doesn't disappoint, as he explains several key fallacies in current education practice that need to be addressed and overhauled.

REFLECTIONS

1. Has your school or district ever invited or coordinated a discussion on the ideal school of the future?
2. What current schooling practices do you feel are outdated, or not in the best interest of children and youth?
3. What resources are truly essential in facilitating an effective classroom?

Chapter Eleven

Christmas Surprise

Those who are carrying the organization are often so good and selfless at what they do, others hardly notice . . . until one day, they're gone.

Life lesson: Don't delay in planning special and unique celebrations for members of the organization who have quietly served. They are the very cornerstone.

John and Marge invited Brad and his wife, Liz, over for a relaxing evening during Christmas break. John was not supposed to do much extra during the holidays, but Marge knew this would do him good.

"Come on into the parlor, folks. Let's have some hot tea while Marge finishes with getting supper ready." Liz followed Marge into the kitchen to assist, as John found the couch and leaned back with a sigh. Brad sat in the closest chair, but seemed distant.

"What's wrong, son?"

"Oh, I don't want to bother you during your Christmas season with this, John. Just a matter down at school that caught me off guard."

"Oh goodness, Brad. You know I'm not going to be bothered by any of your many school adventures. That's what I'm here for, remember?"

"Well, that's true. You *are* my mentor. . . . OK, but I'll be brief."

"What's on your mind?"

"Mrs. Stephenson called me on the last day of fall semester last week and told me that she did not want anyone to know, but she's retiring."

"Smith School's secretary?"

"Yep. And I'm sick over it, John. I don't have the heart to tell Millie. It would've been bad enough if Mrs. Stephenson would have retired under my watch last year, or when I come back next year. But, right now, with all that Millie has on her plate, I just don't know how that school will survive."

"It will be a difficult blow, Brad. Few people realize the huge role school secretaries play. In reality, they should not be called *secretaries.* What an inaccurate description. I know for me, over the years, my secretary was for all intents and purposes the school manager. And how she conducted herself every day, how she ran the office, how she fielded phone calls, complaints, knew what child went with what parent, met the variety of needs of our teachers and other staff, kept me organized and headed in the right direction . . . well, you get my point. A good school secretary is priceless.

"In fact, Brad, a secretary can make or break a school. Good secretaries should be paid two or three times their salary. And, to be frank, bad secretaries need to be gotten out of that office just as soon as possible, 'cause they are doing daily damage to the school's reputation."

"I have to agree, John. And, you've given me an idea for our next cadre session. I need to emphasize what you just explained, and make sure our group has a very transparent conversation about whether any of them need to move someone out of their front office. It's not fair to the kids, the staff, or the community. . . . But, in the mean time, help me figure out how to express to Mrs. Stephenson just how much she has meant to our school and entire school district over the years."

"She's not even going to come back for one last day?"

"She told me over the phone that this was a tough decision, and that she wanted to leave the school without any emotional stuff. Apparently, she felt like the end of the fall semester was the best time."

"What will the staff say?"

"Oh, mercy, John . . . the staff, the students, the parents, the community— they all will be killed over this. Mrs. Stephenson in many ways *is* Smith School. She understands servant leadership perhaps better than anyone else in our district. She is tirelessly patient, and gentle, and kind. She makes everyone who walks in that office feel special—feel like they're important and truly appreciated by the school."

"Then she needs a special send off, not only for her to receive the proper respect she deserves from the entire school community, but also so all of you can celebrate with her and have the right kind of closure. Sounds like she's an institution . . . a pillar."

"She's even more than that, John. She's all that's good about any organization."

"Then tell her so."

"But how? School's out for two weeks, and she's already cleaned her desk out. She made it clear that she does *not* want to come back to school for one last time."

"Where does she go to church?"

"Hey, John, that's an idea! What if we worked with her pastor and I could somehow bring the Smith School staff to her church one Sunday during Christmas?"

"I'd go one better. I'd invite the whole town."

"To church?"

"To church, after church, all afternoon—just make it Mrs. Stephenson's day all day long—for the entire community. Sing to her in worship; let the sermon be centered around her servant's heart; let students shower her with gifts as part of a reception for the public. Make it the most special retirement celebration this town's ever seen."

"I'm going to do it, John."

"Good, son. We spend so much time in life running around taking care of the little things, while letting the big things slip right on by without hardly a whisper. Too often, they are 'moments in time' that won't be coming around again."

"I'm learning so many 'gold nuggets' about life from you, John. It's as if you view things differently—as if you're looking down from above, from outside your world." Brad realized the delicate nature of what he had said even before the words left his mouth.

"More than you would know, son . . . more than you would know."

In The Heart of a Leader, *Ken Blanchard (1999) shares the core values of goodness, and how a leader's focus on the heart and relationships defines the organization.*

SUMMARY

The secretary of Smith School is retiring, and Brad is distraught and at a loss for what to do. John helps devise a plan that will honor this pillar of the community, who has modeled servant leadership to all she's come in contact with over the years.

REFLECTIONS

1. How does your school honor those who are leaving, or retiring?

2. What role does your school secretary play in the culture of your school?
3. How does your principal, school council, or school district select the staff who run the office in your school?

Chapter Twelve

Inspire, Equip, Let Go

The prince kept his thumb on the kingdom, so afraid he'd lose control. One day, he left on a journey, and he worried that his people would not know what to do while he was gone. Instead, they cheered and laughed, and worked as if a load had been lifted . . . they could breathe again.

Life lesson: The assigned role of "leader" is intoxicating, and can lead to addiction to power, manipulation, and a controlling nature that is stifling to others. Simply put, these traits are the very opposite of servant leadership.

January brought with it bitter cold and snow, and Brad wondered if John's doctor would let him have any visitors. But instead, Marge had called and asked Brad to come by. "He's got cabin fever, Brad. Could you take him for a snow hike? The doctor said if you don't have a cold, it should be OK."

"I don't have any sniffles or fever as far as I know, Marge. I'd love to get out and play in the snow a little myself. I'll be right over."

As Brad drove up in his four-wheel-drive pickup, John was waiting, and almost ran out the door. "Buddy, I'm so glad to see you! Marge and I can only do so many jigsaw puzzles the kids got us for Christmas, before I start to need the outdoors again."

"Know what you mean, John. Let's take a drive and do some hiking on an old trail I used to explore as a kid."

"Yes, sir, I'm game for it—let's go!"

Brad had not seen John feeling this good in a long time, and he was encouraged that maybe the treatments were stopping the cancer in its tracks. "Got a question for you, John. One of the principals I'm working with this year, a lady who's been at her middle school for about three years, keeps making the same mistakes over and over, and I'm afraid her staff is going to turn on her soon if she doesn't make some personal adjustments."

"How do you mean?"

"Well, to put it bluntly—she's just too bossy."

"Certainly a common ailment of supervisors, Brad, and not just in the education sector either. What have you addressed with her so far?"

"Well, I have her reading a good book that details how to build shared leadership in the organization, and I finally got her to attend our last cadre meeting."

"Good, that's a huge step for her right there."

"What she seems to be lacking, John, is an accurate picture of how controlling she is with her staff."

"Have you observed this, Brad?"

"Oh, definitely. The last time I was visiting her school, she was explaining something to me, and she suddenly called her assistant into the office. She gave him a mile-long list of details she needed taken care of that day, but then proceeded to tell him how to do every little thing. It upset me and I don't even work for her."

"Was she polite to him? Maybe she's doing some coaching herself."

"Well, no, she wasn't polite. She didn't even introduce him to me. And no, John, I don't see her coaching *anybody*. What I have observed over and over is her endless micro-managing of people—from office staff, to teachers, to students. The other day she was even on the phone with the mayor, who was scheduled to come and speak to a class that week. But, he needed to re-schedule. The way she talked down to him, it was so abrasive, like the way a big sister would talk to a little brother when frustrated over something. . . . It was . . ."

"Unprofessional?"

"You took the word right out of my mouth, John. Yes, to be honest, it was very unprofessional."

"What can we do, Brad?"

"I'm not sure. I'd sure like for her to just walk around one day and observe a principal with an entirely different approach."

"Who do you have in mind?"

"Well, there's a lady who's doing some absolutely marvelous things with a school about two hours from here. She'd be perfect."

"Then do it."

"Oh, but I don't think my bossy principal will go. She's so unaware of how she grates on people's nerves with her controlling attitude."

"Then you will have to tell her."

"What?"

"Sometimes, the mentor has to break the bad news, if the pupil has any hope of getting better."

"I know, John, but you don't know this person. She will then proceed to set me straight, and show me the door."

"Didn't you just say that you think her staff has just about had enough?"

"Yes, I'd say if they were told right now that they were going to be assigned a new principal, they'd welcome the change tomorrow—without even asking who it might be."

"Does she know her stuff—I mean, instructionally, the big picture?"

"That's what's so sad, John. She has the technical skills to be a great principal. I'm sure she could write books that would be helpful to other principals. But in the area of emotional intelligence, relationships, servant leadership . . . she's just lost."

"What would you tell her if she would actually listen, and not throw you out the door?"

"Well, I'd start by asking her if she's surveyed her staff recently. Then, I'd help her develop a survey tool that would allow all of the employees of that school, and volunteers, too, to give input as to what is working well, but what is also lacking."

"What would be lacking?"

"Oh, guaranteed, the staff would overwhelmingly ask her to back off, and let them do their jobs."

"What would you then tell her, as her mentor?"

"I'd simply ask her to start spending time communicating her vision in a more inspiring, less intimidating way. Then I'd ask her to focus on empowering and equipping her staff—with a shift from telling them everything they need to be doing to giving them broad goals, and then stepping back and letting them grow."

Brad opened his hands and spread his arms wide. "I'd ask her to let them go—turn her people loose to be the skilled educators and caregivers that they have been trained to be. She is working so, so hard, but too much on the wrong things. Instead of developing leaders all around her, she's squeezing so tight, she's suffocating them. They don't see her as an inspiring leader, although her internal vision for the school is very strong. They see her as a roadblock, an obstacle who is keeping the school from soaring. It's so sad, John."

"Then go back to that school and do what you just told me you'd like to do."

"No way, John. No way!"

"So, you're just going to let her hang herself, Brad? What type of a mentor is that?"

"But, John, you've never had to go in and tell someone to their face how much of their work was not even respected by their staff."

"Yes I have. . . . Do you remember Todd from last year's cadre sessions?"

"Certainly. One of the finest principals in our region."

"He was drowning in his own self-centeredness when I was assigned to basically give him one more year."

"What did you tell him?"

"The truth."

"Did he listen?"

"Not at first. But I wasn't going anywhere. The superintendent asked for my help, and told me this was strike three for Todd if he didn't respond to my assistance. His attitude stunk, and I remember dreading to have to sit and listen to his excuses—when in reality he knew so little about school leadership."

"You cared enough to help him take a good look in the mirror."

"That's about it. And when he began to realize that leading a school was not about him, but was about serving others, he woke up. It was amazing to watch him change."

"Well, if someone with that bad of an attitude can change, then surely someone who is working too hard can change."

"That's a good way to put it, Brad. Your principal is so sure of what needs to be done to run her school, she's trying to tell everyone in detail every day how it's all supposed to work. That style of management turns people off big time. Yes, her people are probably indeed having trouble breathing. I like the way you put it a minute ago . . . inspire, equip, let go."

"John, I'll try."

"Take her to the other school, Brad. On the way back home, work into the conversation the need to survey her staff. After the results come in, you'll have the data that will help her slow down and listen. She'll need some training on emotional intelligence, and what healthy organizations look like, and how the designated leader plays the key role in allowing for that type of culture to flourish."

"You make it sound so easy, John."

"It is, son. Helping others to discover the wonderful world of servant leadership is the most fulfilling work I've ever done."

"We're here. Ready for a walk in the snow?"

"Let's do it. I even left my cane at home. That stick is such a nuisance!"

In It's Your Ship, *D. Michael Abrashoff (2002) dispels the myth that the best leaders "boss" and micro-manage their way to organizational effectiveness. Instead, he enlightens the reader with true stories of how he inspired, equipped, and then let go.*

SUMMARY

Brad is mentoring a principal with major control problems, and seeks John's advice. John tells Brad that he needs to tell her the truth—however uncomfortable it may be—if he expects to help this lady save her job, and set the school free to grow.

REFLECTIONS

1. Can you think of a time when a well-intentioned "boss" stifled creativity, thus slowing the energy level and progress of the organization?
2. What is the difference in inspiring leadership and micro-managing leadership?
3. Why is it imperative that emotional intelligence be the linchpin in creating healthy organizational culture?

Chapter Thirteen

The Kid from the Other Side of Town

Every now and then, a prodigy comes along. And sometimes, his (her) roots are not from the garden of privilege. Instead, it's as if a miracle has happened. Someone cared, and wouldn't you know it, the kid climbs out of the vicious cycle! Who would have thought it possible?

Life lesson: The kids in our school buildings who are "misfits," or stand on the fringe with blank stares . . . oh, if we had enough adults who saw the potential in these outliers—our society would never be the same.

"How'd your intervention go, Brad?" John fluffed his pillow on the couch, and waited for an answer.

"Intervention?"

"You know—the conversation with the intellectual principal who's bossing herself right out of a job."

"John, I was amazed. She did agree to go visit the school I had recommended. And, she learned from the principal there that she needed to be surveying her staff and students every semester. She's getting ready to begin this process next week. So, we'll see what happens. The only thing I've cautioned her about thus far is to not be surprised by the feedback—as seeing ourselves through the eyes of others can be humbling, but also very helpful."

"Wonderful, Brad! Now you will be able to help her. Good work!"

"I wouldn't have approached the issue until the end of the year, if not for your insistence that I stop being afraid, and simply do the right thing. If I had waited to June, it might have been too late."

"Still could be, Brad. Make sure you stay on top of this, and coach her aggressively after those surveys come back. If she's willing to listen, and work on her weak areas, who knows how quickly the staff will respond by giving her time and lots of grace."

"I know, John. I'm on it, and I'm excited for what can come of this long term for her, and for that school. . . . I have some other exciting news I wanted to share with you. Millie called me earlier this morning, and she just found out that Smith School has a kid who has been accepted to Princeton. First Ivy League school for anyone in this town ever. How about those apples?"

"You gotta be joking, Brad! Who's the student?"

"Eliza Bellomy."

"Ol' Ike's granddaughter?"

"Yep. Seems she had been writing poems and short stories for years, and keeping a journal at home of her family's life in poverty. No one at school had paid much attention to her creative writing talents, except to give her A's and move her along. Finally, this summer, as she met with the counselor to map out a strategy for possibly going to college, something finally registered. The counselor placed her in the advanced English class, the literary club, and put her on the student newspaper and yearbook staff. But, the biggest change happened on the first day of school."

"How so?"

"Because on the first day of school, Mrs. Nicholson started her first year as a teacher at Smith School."

"Who's Mrs. Nicholson?"

"She and her husband moved here with his work. We had an English opening, and Dr. Cobb hired her. He had checked with her former school system, and the leadership there gave her rave reviews. They told Dr. Cobb that there was no finer English teacher anywhere, because of how she took the kids under her wing and made her subject come alive."

"Sounds like a teacher any principal would love to have walk through the door. I bet Millie is thrilled."

"Yes, for Eliza, and for all the students in Mrs. Nicholson's classes. Millie shared with me that when she has observed in her classroom, it's as if time stops. She reads to the kids, like back in elementary school days. She has them doing drama to make the literature relevant. She reads her own poetry, too, and she opens up the floor for students to express their creative juices in an accepted, nonpressured way. Thus, the kids are even writing songs, and sometimes playing their guitars or other instruments as well. They are currently working on the spring play, which will be open to the community. I can't wait to see what they've come up with. You and Marge must come see it, John."

"Oh, we will, Brad. I'd love to meet Mrs. Nicholson. I want to get to know this talented person who my grandkids may have as a teacher some day. Teachers who have a passion for their work, and who genuinely love kids and can connect with them—these are the cream of the crop that we should be going after every time we have a teaching vacancy. Great teaching builds great schools. Great schools build great communities. Great communities are the only way to build a great society. . . . Tell me more about this Eliza girl. Her granddad was a dear friend, and ran his garbage route right by our front door for years and years."

"Well, John, it seems that Ike became a heavy drinker after he retired. Had never touched the stuff before he was finally laid off. But the depression of sitting around doing nothing all day drove him to hanging with buddies who loved to bring liquor to their card games. His health went down hill, and his alcoholism eventually killed him. Eliza has shared with Millie that what she saw her family go through during Ike's last years made her vow to never have to live not knowing how the bills were going to be paid. So, she's not scared of going to Princeton—a long way from home. She realizes this is her big chance to climb out, and she's going for it."

"How many more Elizas do we have down at Smith School right now, Brad? I know how hard your staff was working last year to reinvent that school so that it was focused on the varying needs of each student, and finally letting go of the parts of the old traditional model that don't work well."

"You mean, how many kids do we have who have a hidden talent locked up inside, and they're not sure if they have the courage or a way to dig deep to find it and let it out? Oh, I'd say about half of our senior class is in that twilight zone of senior high school where, basically, they could go either way. Some will realize that they must keep learning, and will go on to post-secondary of some kind. But, even with all we're doing to mentor, to advise, to meet their needs one to one, there's still way too many who will not *get it* until it's too late, after they've made some terrible life choices."

"I know you all have a very effective advisor/advisee program, and you work on the creative arts, with extra physical education, kids working online from home—a very rich and diverse learning culture that is truly a twenty-first-century model for others to learn from. But, Brad, even with all of this support, you feel half of your senior class stand a good chance of making poor life choices in the next few months?"

"Yes, even with our small school, which gives us so many advantages in terms of getting to know the students on a true mentor-pupil relationship level, I know of kids who are falling through the cracks right now. In fact, Eliza was falling through the cracks, John. Without this new teacher and her connecting with Eliza, would she have blossomed this year? Would we have been able to get her to that first day of college? Or, would she have been sucked back into the pit, with the illusion that she might need to get a job first to help support her family, hoping beyond hope she would get to chase her dreams and go on to school later on?"

"So you truly feel that Eliza's life was forever changed, just in time, this past fall when she was set free to focus on her learning passion by someone who cared deeply about her creative genius, but who also cared for her as a person?"

"I'm sure of it, John. At our little school, last year we had thirty seniors. We worked like we never had before to get them focused on going on to more training after high school. I know of ten of those thirty who did not make the bold decision to go for it. They told us they planned to; we helped them with the applications and even took them to visit colleges and vocational schools. But something did not connect."

"Only thirty seniors? I would have thought it would have been higher."

"With that group last year, John, going back to their ninth grade year, about twenty percent dropped out."

"Even at this little community school, where everyone knows your name?"

"Yep. Oh—it's much higher across the board in our state, and nationally, too."

"I know. I've seen those statistics and have preached sermons about this crisis, too. I just assumed we were finally closing the gap at least a little in the area of dropouts."

"Well, we are—slightly."

"Slightly is not near good enough. No kid in this generation of opportunity should even be thinking of dropping out of school. It's a black eye on our society and how we have run our education system, Brad."

"But Smith School and many others are making progress, John."

"Yes, but you know what, Brad? Even one kid dropping out is one too many. None of Smithtown's children should be doomed to such a fate, no matter how ornery they seem to be, or no matter how little support they get at home. And, I'll go one further. Not one of this year's seniors should fall through the cracks. All thirty should right now be living their dream just like Eliza is. Can Millie give you a list of the kids that in reality are still a "maybe" for having sincere plans of going on to postsecondary next year?"

"I'm sure she can. And, it will be ten or so again."

"One third of the senior class."

"Yes, one third."

"Bring them here next Monday morning."

"What?"

"I want all ten of them here for breakfast next Monday morning. And after that, I want one of them to be assigned to me to mentor for the rest of this spring. Give me the one that you think is most likely to throw his life away. . . . And, one more thing. Find nine other adults in this community who care, and match them up with one senior each as well. Let's not lose one kid this time, Brad. Not one."

"I'll have them here next Monday morning, John. All ten. And, I think Millie can help us find the other nine mentors for this spring."

"Well, let's not stop there. After we get this rolling, we need to do the same thing for the freshman class."

"We will, John. I know this community loves its children that much."

Brad reached over and shook John's hand with a firm grip, and did not want to let go. As he stood up to leave, he saw that gleam in John's eye that he'd not seen in a while. And Brad cried. And John laughed and cried. And they both knew that they had just experienced an epiphany. Brad just shook his head as he drove away, with tears rolling down his face, and thought to himself, "Perhaps his last spring, and what does he do? He's going to save a kid . . . no, ten kids." And Brad prayed, "Dear Lord, please don't take him from us so soon."

In Differentiated Instructional Strategies, *Gayle H. Gregory and Carolyn Chapman (2002) lay out a variety of helpful ideas and a process that assists teachers in adjusting their classrooms to the needs of each student.*

SUMMARY

Smithtown School produces its first Ivy League student—a senior who has overcome growing up on the "poor side of town." John and Brad develop a plan that will allow for one-to-one mentoring of all of the school's at-risk seniors, realizing that one caring adult makes all the difference.

REFLECTIONS

1. Does your school have a coordinated one-to-one adult-to-student mentoring program?
2. Can you think of a student you know of who climbed out of the cycle of poverty against all odds? What adult assistance made the difference?
3. What does your school do for at-risk students (those in danger of dropping out of school, or not going on to postsecondary education of some kind)?

Chapter Fourteen

Tough Love

The mentor looked the pupil square in the eye, and simply said, "I care for you too much to let you take the wide and easy road. No, son, you're going to walk the road less traveled. Yes, it will be rough. Yes it will be scary. Yes, it will be lonely at times. But at the end of that journey, you will find your dream."

Life lesson: We rarely forget those who down through our lives have seen something in us we perhaps didn't even see in ourselves. Schools with aggressive one-to-one mentoring programs for *all* students realize this key principle of a personal coaching relationship.

John hadn't slept well the night before, as he thought about the kids who were coming to visit him the next morning. He was up before dawn, helping Marge with breakfast. "Now you just go sit down, John. I'll take care of the kitchen."

"I know, I know. But Marge, I just want them to have such a good morning. Think what they must think, being dragged over here in a school van to meet someone they don't even know, who's sick and down on the couch."

"Oh mercy me, John! You're just nervous 'cause you know high school kids often pretty much have the final say if they really want to. So, be prepared. You may be ignored this morning, after all is said and done."

"They won't have the final say this time, Marge. Too much riding on these next few months of their schooling."

"Just remember, they're kids."

"That's my point exactly."

The van drove up, and out popped Brad, Millie, and ten high school seniors—six girls and four boys.

"Come in, come in! My, what a fine-looking crew! If you're from Smithtown School, I know you're top of the line. . . . My wife, Margie, has a hot breakfast for everyone, so make your way to the kitchen."

John did not feel as tired as usual, and had dressed in jeans and a sweatshirt. He sat down at the head of the table, and just listened as the chatter picked up and everyone enjoyed a delicious meal.

Finally, Brad made the segue to the real reason they were all there. "Guys, this is John, my mentor. He's one of the coolest, brightest, caring people I have ever known. He and I have been talking about how well our mentoring program for principals is going, and have tossed around the idea that perhaps our senior class could benefit from such a program. So, guess who's been selected to be in the first pilot group?"

John cleared his throat, and simply asked, "Who wants to share with me your dream?" Everyone just looked around the table at each other.

"Let me put it another way," John added. "If you could plan out the ideal future for yourself, what would it be?"

One girl, who was sitting next to Marge, spoke up. "I would love to go on to college and study medicine."

Another girl added, "I'm thinking about beautician's school, but what I'd really love to do is study interior design."

"I'd love to travel."

"I'd love to work with horses."

"I've always dreamed of going to law school."

"I've thought about seminary."

John smiled, and asked the boys to jump in. "Guys, how about you? What's your dream?"

Finally, a sandy-haired fella, thin and still eating everything he could get his hands on from the leftovers, blurted out, "I'd love to run my own car business." A couple of the other boys grinned, and nodded in agreement.

"What about you?" John looked down at the end of the table, to his left. There sat a tall, dark-haired young man with a scowl on his face.

"I'm going to work at my granddaddy's farm, just like my Uncle Ned. And I don't need no education to do that. I know more about livestock, and tractors, and raising crops than anyone else at school anyway. Besides, they don't even have courses in college for farmers."

"Oh yes they do." John spoke softly and smiled. "I didn't catch your name, son. What should I call you?"

"Just call me JR—which is short for Junior."

"Well, JR, there's a whole new fascinating world out there for people who love agriculture like you seem to." JR just slumped further down into his chair, and looked at his glass of milk.

One of the girls spoke up. "Sir, I'd love to go on to school after I graduate this year, but my folks can barely afford to pay for my yearbook. I couldn't ask them to fork out that type of money. They'd have to borrow so much they'd never be able to pay for it."

"Oh, but there's scholarships, and grants, and low-interest loans that you don't even have to begin paying on until you're out of school. Plus, there's work study options, where you work part-time while on campus to help offset your tuition. I promise every one of you—if you will let us work with you this spring, having conversations just like we're doing here, you can go on to school next fall."

Some of the kids smiled, and shifted in their chairs. JR just grunted. "Did you say something, JR?" John knew this was crunch time, as JR could very easily steer the group away from thinking about the possibilities.

"No. Just was thinking how silly and weird it would be for all of us to have breakfast every week like this to talk about stuff that ain't gonna happen."

"Oh, we won't keep meeting as a group. Well, perhaps the week after you graduate this spring. But mostly, we're going to have a personal mentor for each of you—an adult who cares so much about you and your dreams, that this person will walk you through every step of the way. . . . Even take you to visit the schools you'd like to know more about, and also help you with filling out applications."

The kids all looked around, with big bright eyes, as if to say, "Is this some kind of a practical joke?"

John knew what they were thinking, and quickly added, "Every year, here in Smithtown, and all across the country, we have our pomp and circumstance high school graduations, and everyone assumes that the seniors who have made it across that stage are on their way to a life of fulfillment and use of the talents they've been blessed with. But in reality, a large number of those graduating seniors never get past thinking about what they really should be doing next. Somehow, our system has left them stranded. Somehow, they don't know how to cross that bridge to their dreams. So this year, with you ten as our first pilot group, that's going to change at Smithtown."

One of the girls stood up and clapped her hands, as she squealed with excitement. Simultaneously, the others stood up, too. Marge, who had been sitting at the other end opposite John, got tears in her eyes, and just nodded to John as if to say, "You did it, Honey. They believe you."

And Brad looked at his shoes and shook his head from side to side, while thinking, "The master has done it again. He's pulled another rabbit out of the hat. He's ignited another fire."

But JR didn't stand. Instead, he threw his hat down in disgust, crossed his arms, and simply muttered, "I ain't doing any of this nonsense. I'm staying home, and I'm going to farm."

"Fine JR. I'll mentor you this spring, get to know you better, take you on a fishing outing or two, let you show me where the best farms in the county are, then after summer rolls around, if you still don't think you need to give it a try, I'll let it go. Deal?"

JR picked up his hat, and reached for another pancake. "I guess so."

"Super," added John. "Now, next week, for starters, JR, you and I are going to visit the school of agriculture at the state university. Millie, may we borrow the school van?"

Millie had been mostly stunned during all of this very intense and potentially life-changing conversation, and she simply said, "Yes, by all means. If you're going to the university, I think I have a couple of other seniors who'll want to tag along."

"Excellent. . . . Well, you all keep chatting, and eating, while I go help Marge stir up some more pancakes. I haven't felt this good in months. I'm starved."

In 9 Things You Simply Must Do, *Henry Cloud (2004) probes the secrets that separate those who live lives of fulfillment, and those who never seem to get there.*

SUMMARY

Millie and Brad bring to John's house the ten seniors who they have identified as high risk for not going on for further schooling after high school. Marge and John feed them breakfast, and John outlines a pilot mentoring program they will be taking part in, before they graduate, with caring adults from the community.

REFLECTIONS

1. What is the process in your school for helping students to identify and cultivate their unique gifts and abilities?
2. If your school district's high school(s) does not have a 100 percent graduation rate, why not? Does your data go back to the freshman year?
3. If some seniors do not go on to postsecondary of some kind, what can the school do to close this gap in the future?

Chapter Fifteen

Meltdown

Those who have the most authority often know the least about what is best for the organization. Thus, eventually, implosion occurs.

Life lesson: When adults find themselves in opposition to each other, they are much harder to reconcile than children. Thus, looking for the "third answer" is a critical step in bringing healing and a culture of "wellness."

The new mentoring program was going great, as Millie found nine additional volunteers to join John in his project. And, JR was loving the time John was devoting to him, especially the after-school fishing outings. John's energy level was strong presently, and he loved what he was feeling—like his old self again. As he came in for lunch after a morning outside, Marge met him at the door.

"Honey, Brad called earlier while you were working in the flower beds. He needs you to talk to Mrs. Petry—the controlling middle school principal. Something's come up at her school and he's out of town. Brad wondered if you could meet with her today. He apologized about this, and left directions just in case you're feeling up to it. And, he emphasized that if you *don't* feel like it, he'll be in tomorrow afternoon and can take care of it then."

"I'll call her right now. I've not been to a school to chat one to one with a principal all year. I'll be glad to get back in the rat race!"

As John introduced himself to Mrs. Petry's secretary, she jumped up and clasped his hand. "Halleluia, I'm so glad you came. She's in her office crying. Oh, it's just been awful here this morning."

"Mrs. Petry?" John gently walked into the office, and shut the door behind him. "I'm John, Brad's friend. He asked me to fill in for him today. How can I help?"

"Oh, sir, Brad has talked so much about you. He thinks so highly of you. You didn't have to come."

"I wanted to. This is what I do—provide support for fellow principals. I used to do this job myself . . . lead a school. Not easy, is it?"

Mrs. Petry put her hands on her desk, and stood up as her voice quivered. "No, it's not what I thought it would be. I just pictured something a whole lot less emotional—more about instruction and learning. But, I've found out the hard way that it's mostly about people and their moods and needs. Sadly, I'm not good in that area."

"Don't be too hard on yourself, Mrs. Petry. No one has the peculiarity of the human condition figured out yet. And I'm afraid we're putting more on you principals of this generation than you can reasonably bear. . . . Now, what do you need to discuss? I'm all ears."

The tall, large-boned lady, with her fair complexion and wearing a business suit, sat back down and simply said, "I resigned this morning."

"Oh, my. Here just a few weeks before school is out? What led to this decision?"

"It's been building up for a while. Brad may have told you that I've been dealing with a staff that is not supporting my management style. Well, this morning, in a short staff meeting I called before school, one of my veteran teachers who has been challenging me a lot lately stood up to me toe to toe over a minor issue in front of the whole group. When I didn't agree with her approach to the problem we were discussing, she abruptly stomped out— saying she's had it and is taking sick days for the rest of the year."

"Well, perhaps that's not a bad thing. Perhaps she's going through a major emotional meltdown herself right now—just as you are. . . . Have you called her at home to talk?"

"No, sir. She left me hanging without even having a sub lined up. I'll never call her, and hope to never speak to her again!"

"Well, just remember, as the principal, you are the one looked to to show maturity in these matters. Just something to think about before you send any long-term messages to the staff about all of this. . . . I'm curious—why did you decide to resign this morning?"

"Because no one is going to talk to me like that, show me up in front of a group, and then brag about it behind my back for the next three years! That's when she can retire, and I can't work with her that long, John. I've just gotta get out of here!"

"Do you want to resign, Mrs. Petry?"

"All I want is to be able to come to work every morning, do my job, help this school become a stronger instructional center, and then go home every evening. I love my work—much of the time. But I can't handle babysitting adults anymore . . . just can't do it."

"Is that how you see it? *Babysitting* other adults?"

"Frankly—yes. This job would be so rewarding, so fulfilling—if not for my staff! I've never seen such a bunch of whiners in my life!"

"Yes, educators can be wound pretty tight sometimes—especially this time of year, as the summer gets closer and closer, and the staff and the students get tired and need a break. . . . Tell me, what have you done lately to give the staff a fresh pat on the back? Any after-school get-togethers, or birthday parties coming up on the calendar?"

"Oh, you sound just like Brad. I don't have time for that wishy-washy stuff, John! This is a school! We are adults! I already did what Brad suggested, and passed out surveys to my staff. And to be honest, they said a bunch of nothing. No one gave me credit for raising our test scores, or how orderly the school runs. All they wanted to do was write about our *culture*. One survey even said something like, 'I'd like to come to work feeling warmth and celebration in a community of people, like how you feel at a wedding or in a flower shop. Instead, I hate this place. It's like coming to work in a prison.' Now tell me, John, how can I work in an environment like this? Flower shop?!!! They've got to be kidding!"

"But, Mrs. Petry, read between the lines. What she is saying is the ambiance here is not good. It's not a friendly place for other adults to work. It's not a positive, relaxed atmosphere. At least to this one staffer, it's a very unhappy place."

"Well, she can join the crowd. Because with attitudes like hers, that's how I feel, too!"

"What would you say if I volunteered to come back tomorrow, and simply walk around taking notes? Then, I would share with you what I observed . . . your strengths, your weaknesses, staff attitudes—good and bad—what I noticed in the classrooms in regard to how students are working and learning. Before you step away from such important work, and what you've invested so much of your life into, could you just put your decision on hold, and let me spend some time in this school?"

"On one condition, sir. You then meet after school tomorrow with my staff and share with them your findings. Because, I'm not up to doing that. But, perhaps they will listen to you."

"I will—if you will make two phone calls for me right now. First, call the superintendent and un-do your resignation for the time being at least. And two, call your teacher who walked out this morning and explain to her that you and I need her here tomorrow—on her regular schedule with her students. And, if you can, bring yourself to apologize or at least be civil with her."

"Why does she need to be here?"

"Because she needs to hear what I have observed after my all-day 'walk through' tomorrow . . . and she needs to accept responsibility. But, she also needs an 'open door,' a way to undo her rash decision this morning. You don't need her laying out the rest of the year—that will hurt the entire school community. And, deep down, I doubt she really wants to."

"I can be civil."

"OK. See you in the morning at 7 AM."

In Teams That Succeed, *the Harvard Business Review (2004) offers several scenarios for developing an effective working culture, including the necessities of emotional intelligence, creativity, and decision making.*

SUMMARY

Brad is out of town, and John is needed in addressing a crisis with a controlling principal. When he arrives at the school, he finds one teacher has already left for home, and the principal has resigned. What he suggests as a solution is surprising, but just might work.

REFLECTIONS

1. Have you ever been witness to a crisis at work that has involved the meltdown of a working relationship between two employees?
2. What did the leadership do to defuse the situation?
3. Why is working for "win, win" so critical in the aftermath of these blowups?

Chapter Sixteen

Putting All the Cards on the Table

Sometimes, the best healing takes place when all the truth is brought to the surface—and everyone's feelings are heard without fear of retribution.

Life lessons: Schools often have dysfunctional cultures, and are not friendly, trusting places to work.

When John arrived at Mrs. Petry's school the next morning, she met him at the door. "I've left a note in every staff person's mailbox, explaining that you would be here today to observe, and that we will have a meeting after school. I also sent them an e-mail on this. So, whatever you need, let me know. I'll have snacks in my office, and I can call out for lunch for you if you wish."

"No, I'll eat in the cafeteria with the kids. But thanks, Mrs. Petry. I'll be in and out all day, so just go about your usual work. Don't let me distract you—I need to see what the typical day here looks like."

"I understand. . . . And thanks again, John. I feel good about this."

"Well, there's an opportunity here for some new beginnings. So, we'll see."

As John spent the morning mingling all over the school's campus, including observing early-morning bus drop-off, breakfast in the cafeteria, PE class outside, how the morning announcements were presented, how students changed classes, one constant kept coming to the surface: This was a school just going through the motions. There seemed to be no life, or spontaneity. Everything seemed to be a rehearsed routine that had happened dozens of times before. And, the classrooms were the same. They seemed more like factories, where workers were mindlessly performing tasks without even thinking about why they were doing it.

At lunch, John sat down with five eighth graders. As he listened to their perceptions of their school, he became enraged inside. "So this is what we've come to?" he thought to himself as he listened to the lack of passion for learning, lack of excitement, lack of respect for the school staff.

In the afternoon, John spent his time interviewing teachers who were on planning time, and then went back to the office and observed how it was run. When the kids had been dismissed for the day, and the buses pulled out, he realized he had more than enough in his notes for the meeting after school. In fact, he realized he had more than enough after the first hour that morning.

When Mrs. Petry introduced him to her staff, John put his notebook down, smiled and began, "First of all, thank you for inviting me in today. I have cancer, and to have the opportunity to be in a school all day long at least one more time is a blessing I never thought I'd have earlier this year. So, this has been special."

And then John's voice broke. "But, I must say, I have been more than just a little surprised all day at how infected this school is. And what I mean by infected is—there seems to be no passion . . . from anyone. When I spoke to the bus drivers this morning, a couple just grunted. When I went outside for PE on this beautiful spring day, half the kids were sitting in the bleachers, staring at the others who were halfway playing what could have been an exciting game of softball.

"When I went into classrooms, I'm not sure I even one time saw a teacher or a student truly enjoying learning. I saw no exciting discussion or debate. I saw no expression of creativity, such as a student sharing a PowerPoint or recent painting or journal entry. In many classes, it seemed worksheets were the rage. Also in many classes, it seemed a couple of kids had a way of keeping the rest of the class distracted. In a few classes, I even noticed that students were sleeping, or sitting looking mindlessly into space or out the window—bored out of their minds. In fact, I would say that a high percentage of the students I observed this morning were bored out of their minds.

"And at lunch, when I sat down with some students to chat? Wow, I was blown away by their lack of ability to discuss anything about school in a positive vein. These were your eighth graders, on their way to high school next year. So, they've been with you for three years. These are the students you hope are selling your school to others in the community, and who will represent you well at the high school. Well, guess what? They think this school is a joke. They seem to have no plan for what high school can mean for their transition on into higher ed or other postsecondary education.

"Furthermore, they say you all have missed the boat on using technology in the classroom. They say you've not challenged them. They say you've used a cookie-cutter approach that anybody could do if simply wanting to manage a group of teenagers for fifty minutes every day."

"And, the lunch conversation was not that far off, because my afternoon interviews with staff revealed similar concerns and gaps. To put it bluntly, you, as a school, have lost your way in terms of what a twenty-first-century classroom should look like, and the rich engagement that should be going on in every room every day.

"Then I wrapped up my day by hanging out in the office. First of all, your outer office personnel need to be taught how to answer the phone in a friendly and professional manner, and they need to be taught how to greet parents and visitors as well. I felt intimidated, and I was just sitting there in the corner out of the way. I can't imagine how it would feel if a parent or grandparent on the receiving end of the conversation.

"Finally, I went in to Mrs. Petry's office. To my amazement, she was doing clerical work that the secretary should have been doing. And, she was taking phone call after phone call from you folks in the classroom over this after-school meeting. I'm not sure who was teaching your classes while you were trying to get out of this meeting, but it was a disappointment to see you taking up your principal's time in this way. It reminded me of the students you teach here—junior high.

"So, here's the deal. You people are going to have to start over. Mrs. Petry, you're going to have to lead the charge in these people starting over. This is not a model school—by any definition. This is a traditional, uninspiring, status quo, 'let's don't rock the boat, or the students might wake up' baby-sitting service in many ways. No wonder you all can't stand it here. Neither can your students. Neither could I—and I've just experienced your culture for a few hours."

John's voice raised, and he felt his hands shaking, but he wasn't going to stop now. "And that's the issue—your culture. Your announcements this morning sounded like those one might hear in a hospital. I kept waiting for a "code blue." This place, for lack of a better analogy, makes me think of a prison. In fact, I could take you to a modern-day penal facility here in the United States and show you students who would be much more engaged and learning real-life lessons in their classes. And I promise—I am not exaggerating.

"Here's what I strongly recommend, and then I'm going to leave and let you all talk among yourselves some. It is obvious to me that you have not had any *real* conversation about how to improve your school in a long, long time. You need to not just make some changes. You need to start over. You need to develop a plan of action this spring, and then in June, as soon as the kids go home for the summer, totally reinvent this school. Starting with the master schedule, how to use instructional technology every day in every classroom, manners and morale of all staff—including bus drivers and clerical workers—how to turn your lesson plans into discovery learning—not "sit and get" learning. . . . You just need to start over.

"And in reality, some of you will not want to take on this task, and will ask to transfer, or you may realize it's time to retire. And that's OK—do it. Some will ask for a new principal. Well, perhaps that's what Mrs. Petry will hope for, too, but I will tell you something. Don't blame all of this on Mrs. Petry. This is a toxic culture that everyone needs to take some responsibility for allowing to fester over the years. I doubt all of this has developed in the short three years Mrs. Petry has been on her watch.

"Those of you who would like to stay and transform this school are asking yourselves where to start. Before you make even one adjustment, you will need to visit the best schools you can afford to go to, and interview the principals and best teachers in those schools. And, do your research and build into your new model not just strategies, but also the absolute best strategies for what is truly spot on for how kids learn. And I can guarantee you, the research will tell you that you absolutely must create classrooms that focus on lots and lots of creativity and experiential learning—not endless hours of seat work.

"Now, I must go. Thank you so, so much for being attentive listeners. That's the first and most important part of addressing needed change. I am quite sure you all, or most all of you, are dedicated teachers who truly do want what's best for kids. It's just that you don't have a very good school here. It's an outdated, ineffective, 'top-down' model . . . in every way. I wouldn't send my grandkids here and I bet many of you wouldn't send yours here either."

In Methods That Matter, *Harvey Daniels and Marilyn Bizar (1998) offer six structures for best practice classrooms, reminding practitioners that there are better ways to maximize student engagement and success that go far beyond our comfort zones and past teaching models.*

SUMMARY

John spends a day at a middle school, going beneath the surface culture to assist a principal who is ineffective, and on the verge of quitting. In the after-school staff meeting to de-brief, John unloads on the mediocrity he observed all day long, and urges the entire staff not just to modify but also to reinvent this school.

REFLECTIONS

1. Have you ever actually spent an entire day simply observing the holistic culture of another school?
2. What does your school do to address, and then change, obsolete or mediocre classroom practices?
3. Does your school staff routinely discuss gaps or toxicity in the school culture?

Chapter Seventeen

"Heart Transplant" . . .

The truth can hurt so much that those closest to the situation cannot see the reality. Often, they need to step aside, and let new faces and fresh ideas take the organization to the next level.

Life lesson: A wise and experienced coach, not swayed by personal bias or political correctness, can help an organization make great strides toward transformation and renewal. His fresh lens is often the catalyst to long-term positive change.

When Brad returned from his trip, he immediately came over to John's house to discuss the Petry situation. John was sitting on his front porch, enjoying a gentle spring rain, and reading from his Bible.

"John, my man. What have you done? Mrs. Petry says her superintendent is going nuts, as not one, not five, but ten of her staff are demanding transfers. Another five are retiring. My dear friend, can you explain?"

"Sure. I told them the truth."

"Told who the truth?"

"Mrs. Petry and her entire staff—in the teacher's meeting after school on the day I spent with them watching them *not* teach, *not* understand positive school culture, and *not* seem to be able to grasp treating me or anyone else as a customer. I started to call you at lunch and share that I felt Mrs. Petry indeed needed a change of scenery, but the more I thought about it, I realized that would not be the answer. The whole school needs a heart transplant, not just the principal."

"That bad, huh?"

"Yep, Brad . . . that bad."

"What should I do now?"

"There's nothing you can do, until the staff makes up their mind that they are going to be a school—not a mediocre dumping ground for the community's kids. I've been in some less-than-stellar school environments, Brad, but this one takes the cake."

"Should Mrs. Petry resign?"

"Only if she really wants to. Who's to guarantee that her successor would be able to move that school any further along? At least she has an instructional focus, although I didn't see it in the classrooms. So, she's getting huge resistance by teachers who are basically sending her a message that they will run their classrooms just like they always have. Who's to say the next principal will not run into the same road block?"

"But maybe she's why they're so out of energy, so out of that fire and passion that I see in other schools where real learning is going on, and everyone is on board doing innovative things for the kids and the community."

"Oh, definitely, Mrs. Petry's an issue. She's just not the only issue. After the smoke clears, and you see who really is staying, and who really is transferring or retiring, you will then have an opportunity, Brad, to sit down with the principal, and then later her school council, and then after that the entire staff, and develop a bold school improvement plan that can make all the difference when the kids return to school in the fall. All I did was set the table for you to walk along with them with a true school-change mindset. They've had their blinders on for so long, they needed someone to come in and shake them up. I apologize if you're receiving some heat over this."

"No need to apologize, John. The superintendent knew you did what he's known for a while now needed to happen . . . a reality check. He's just wondering about how to replace the staff if too many do indeed move on."

"That's simple, Brad. Simply go out and find new teachers who are so wanting to prove themselves, and train them the right way the first time."

"The right way?"

"Yes. . . . For too long, we've allowed the tail to wag the dog in education. Teachers are hired, given tenure in four years, and then assume they have a lifetime contract with the same classroom, same school, same district. There's no other profession that allows such unaccountable control of the bottom-line results—which in the case of schools is the preparing of kids well for life. Think about it. How hard would it be to take any mediocre school, and focus on one or two key goals every year, and thus keep getting better and better. . . . What's this school's MO?"

"MO?"

"You know, Brad—modes operandi. What's the year-after-year profile, the repeated habits, rituals, academic gaps, other tendencies?"

"Well, the superintendent told me just this morning that reading scores have always been low, math not much better, and the community involvement is always poor."

"Then those are the three areas that the school needs to be relentless about in changing—by the first day of school. Either the teachers can teach reading and math well, or they can't. The district either changes teachers, or gets them the right type of training, resources, and any other help they need to cross over from this endless madness of making the same mistakes, to achieving as a school that knows how to bring students along well in reading and math."

"Shouldn't be all that hard for them to figure out, should it?"

"Of course not. . . . Now, in regard to the school culture. If they will simply learn how to be friendly with people, to open their school up to the community, to invite in guest speakers and volunteers to be a part of the school, they will see instant increased support from the community. They don't have support because they have sent a clear message they don't want support. Those days should be over by the end of summer break. So, if Mrs. Petry is up to working on this new culture of community and learning, she just might surprise some people once her staff is held more accountable, too. If she's not up to it, then the superintendent needs to find someone who is, and get on with the work of educating kids—not playing to the emotions of the adults in the building."

"We do too much of that in education, don't we, John?"

"Yes, we sure do, Brad. I love teaching—always have, from the time I was in college learning about it, and still do. What I can't understand is why we allow people who don't enjoy it to stay in the classroom, as if it's their privilege or something."

"Weak or mediocre teachers don't leave because of the stable job, pretty good money, and the other perks, John. And principals and district leadership don't ask them to leave because it's just plain ol' not fun to spend so much painful energy and time, and sometimes legal fees, on telling someone they're not very good at what they do."

"But, Brad, listen to what you're saying. So, we choose the cowardly route. . . . We cover up our hiring mistakes by bringing them back every year, instead of getting them intensive mentoring help and training, or giving them the best gift we could give them by setting them free to go on to other meaningful life work they're more suited for."

"I know, I know—it's a crazy, broken system."

"Yes, and guess who are the big losers, Brad?"

"The kids."

"Exactly. The kids."

"But Mrs. Petry's school has an opportunity this summer to do something radically different."

"Yes, they do. They have a rare opportunity to essentially be reborn as a school community—from top to bottom. If I were the superintendent, I'd be jumping for joy. And if I was a parent, I'd be jumping for joy. And Brad, if I was a teacher who truly cared about that school and its children, I'd be jumping for joy."

"You've mentioned the three weak areas you'd focus on as priorities all year. What else would you change, John?"

"The better way to answer that is what I told the staff when I gave them my report. If I were a new principal, or a returning principal, at any school, I'd look at the data, student surveys, staff and parent surveys, and I'd be in re-invention mode. It's so, so exciting to be in the middle of school transformation, and I think too many educators think they're doing it when they're not."

"How do you mean?"

"Brad, tell me what you dislike the most about being a principal. . . . What bogs you down—gets you stressed and disillusioned quicker than anything else?"

"Oh, let's see—for starters, I absolutely hate the adult bickering and emotional levels that too often dominate my day. I don't like all of the endless paperwork. I deeply resent the rigid routine—you know, master schedule glitches but we can't make changes because a computer spits it out for us in the summer and we're stuck with it. I don't like the gaps in the curriculum. . . . Why can't we offer more arts? Why can't we offer more time for PE? Why can't we go on more interesting field trips? These are the very basics of a good holistic, liberal arts education—and we somehow ignore them as if they're not important.

"Why can't we truly do a month-long thematic unit across the curriculum that impacts every child in the school in a positive way? Why can't our accelerated students have independent learning opportunities, or volunteer tutors? Why can't they even do some of their work online at home if the class structure is holding them back? Why can't we celebrate daily successes more?

"Why can't we get away from the bureaucratic nature of school, which does indeed make it seem so uninspiring at times for the kids I'm sure, and just get zeroed in every day on high-quality teaching and learning? It seems too often just so mundane and like an assembly-line profession. And in all fairness, John, that's why teachers sometimes get lost in the maze. They weren't that way when they came to us fresh out of college and hoping to make a difference in the lives of their students."

"And this is what you need to tell Mrs. Petry, Brad. Perhaps she and her entire staff simply need to be set free."

In Winning Through Innovation, *Michael L. Tushman and Charles A. O'Reilly III (2002) provide practical strategies for organizational change and renewal, reminding the reader that this is what healthy and growing organizations do.*

SUMMARY

Brad gets fallout from John's lecture of Mrs. Petry's staff, and he and John discuss the reality of the harm that is caused when teachers don't enjoy their work. John lays out a simple plan for transforming any school with new beginnings and renewal.

REFLECTIONS

1. What barriers in your school have become stumbling blocks to true transformational healing and change?
2. Have you ever been a part of the grassroots planning of the overhaul or reinvention of an organization?
3. What non-negotiables would need to be in place for your school to be reborn between this year and the next?

Chapter Eighteen

The Clique

In many schools, there is a toxic element that most adults don't know how to address—the privileged thinking that casts a dark shadow when a few kids assume the role of "the in crowd." . . . How far this entitlement can go is quite shocking. . . . How adults seem to be paralyzed by it is nauseating.

Life lesson: Some argue that if you remove the ten worst "outcasts" in a school, immediately, the culture will be healthier in a variety of ways. In reality, this can be said for the ten most obnoxious "rich brats" as well. A leader of integrity harnesses these variables in ways that are fair to the entire student body, thus creating a culture of health and accountability—for *all* students.

Brad had volunteered to take John to his cancer doctor for a checkup, and John was all smiles as he fast steps out of the office.

"What did he say this time around?" Brad was so hoping for good news.

"He simply says that he sees no advance, and that possibly we've turned the corner. Let's go get a milkshake. I'm feeling like some celebrating!"

As Brad drove the two in his truck across town, John immediately started talking about their principal project. "You know, son, I've been thinking. We need to build a strand into our program that includes one-day walkthrough evaluations like the one I did for Mrs. Petry's school. That was a powerful exercise, and it can have huge impact on that school if they will get their pride out of the way. By the way, what's the latest on their mass exodus?"

"Good news, John. I've had a couple of great talks with Mrs. Petry. Pretty much challenged her with the *starting over* concept you talked about the other day. She agrees with you, and has decided to stay for one more year. Most of the staff are staying, although there have been three retirements announced and the superintendent has granted three other transfers. And, Mrs. Petry is not renewing two contracts of newer teachers who haven't taken their professional development and personal growth seriously."

"Plus, the superintendent is terminating one tenured teacher who has been moved around from school to school in the district for several years. This fella is a real card, apparently mostly just sits and reads the paper while his social studies and PE classes languish in his permanent study-hall world. The super is expecting a lawsuit, but he has years of documentation on this guy. So, he's sending the message across the district that it's strike three."

"And now, Brad, that school has the opportunity of a lifetime. . . . It should seize this moment in time and do whatever it takes to renew . . . to be reborn."

"And that's what they're working on, John. They took your assessment very, very seriously, and they're embracing the superintendent's charge to do whatever they need to do to truly meet the needs of the kids. It's exciting to see the transformation that is beginning to take shape in that school community. I've never seen so much enthusiasm and smiling faces in what many would call a 'St. Elsewhere' school."

"Wonderful! You've made my day, Brad. . . . Well, you and the doctor, I should say."

"But I've got another problem for you, John. I have a school that is so toxic you can feel it when you walk in the front door—but not because of a dysfunctional staff. Instead, they are being held hostage by a small group of kids that have been allowed to do as they please for so long, they now basically run the school."

"A clique."

"Exactly. And not just your run-of-the-mill group of egotistical kids. The culture in this school is almost fearful, with a dark side to it that is hugely because four or five students are in control."

"How do you mean, Brad? Surely the principal and his leadership team see what's going on, and are doing something to correct it."

"They feel like their hands are tied. These school bosses are the offspring of the town's mayor, county attorney, a couple of doctors, and a millionaire that has given the school district land for a new high school in a couple of years."

"Wow, the ol' barnyard-politics game raises its ugly head. I've seen it all my life, Brad. What have you suggested to the principal in terms of solutions?"

"Oh, it's too late for him. He's retiring this summer. But, his assistant is young, and is not going to allow business as usual. We three met the other day, and he wants a plan in place before school begins this fall that will call the hand of the privileged few, and send a message to the entire student body and school community that he's not tolerating how the school culture has deteriorated due to the school's brat pack."

"Well, good for him! I'd like to meet this young man someday. Does he attend your principals' small group?"

"He sure does, and I'd like to bring this topic to the surface in our next cohort session. What would you recommend in terms of a plan of action that I could share with the whole group? I'm sure other principals are dealing with this issue in varying degrees."

"Well, for starters, Brad, what we're talking about here is control. Every organization deals with it—not just schools. In any setting, a few will eventually try to rise to the top and, however innocently at first, seize power. It just so happens that in some instances, in the school setting, the combination of spoiled control-freak kids and their wealthy and influential parents presents a powder-keg situation where even the teachers, who normally assume much of the power, are intimidated and will succumb to playing the games. It's a bizarre scenario that unfolds, but it is so, so unfair to the other students, and the entire school community. So, due to the human condition of jockeying for power by at least a few, you should start your session with a discussion of this reality."

"Then, explain to your group the core values of servant leadership . . . the whole concept of empowering, equipping, putting others ahead of ourselves and serving instead of bossing—what that means for school community."

"Then, finally, create a model for your principals that will not only allow them to talk about addressing cliques in a school culture, but also provide for them a tool that will diffuse the controlling of the entire school by a few— thus protecting the student body, staff, and community from this type of oppression."

"But what would you include in your model, John?"

"Well, you basically start with how you treat people and expect them to be treated, from the first day of school. And, you don't bend in regards to this staple of character that the whole school soon begins to adopt."

"OK. I'm with you so far. Now, let me give you some examples, and you tell me how you'd handle them with the core values you're talking about here."

"Good—shoot me some real case episodes that would not be in the best interest of a school."

"The president of the student body lobbies the office staff for a pep rally the very first week of school, just because he wants to give a talk about school spirit and what his plans are for getting the student government more involved in the school's policies this year."

"Is he being sincere?"

"Not completely. He has a history of being just far enough away from the scene of the crime that the school has never quite caught him in the act of inciting problems, but the principal does not trust this fella."

"Then why would you ever give him the microphone? The principal needs to simply share that he will have the first pep rally on the school calendar later in the first month of school, and that the first week of school, he does indeed plan to meet with the student council and follow through on the many good ideas they presented to him at the end of the past year."

"OK. Not bad, John. But this teenage leader with an attitude will not just go away so quickly. What would be your next move?"

"My next *move*? It's not a chess game, Brad. I would treat this kid with the respect that I would treat all the other students, and would indeed tap into his leadership skills appropriately. Most likely, he would enjoy the student council brainstorming session, and would have some good ideas. But, in that meeting I would make it clear that I am looking for mature student leaders, who have a positive attitude and who aren't trying to run the school. Then, it would be up to him to earn my confidence, or not."

"Here's another theoretical time bomb waiting to explode. The clique works in the office during their study hall, and seems to have every key leadership position in the school. They and their parents have assumed this was an entitlement that they claimed when they were in elementary school."

"This one's harder in some ways. But, you can't have a healthy school environment, with *every* student feeling appreciated and treated fairly, if the prisoners are running the asylum, so to speak. So, the principal will have to bust up the gang by implementing a new model for how students are assigned to work in the office."

"How would you go about doing that?"

"One way would be to meet with his adult office staff, and share how he wants the office to run under his tenure. Nothing says he has to follow the former plan. It would be better to not have any students working in the office than to allow the clique to continue to run the show. Perhaps allow for *all* upperclassmen who are in good standing with their grades, and who have the free time on their schedule, to apply for office positions. Some of the clique might indeed be selected for the coming year. But, it is highly unlikely all of them would if a democratic and fair process of selection is implemented."

"I like these ideas, John. They're fair, they're in line with what I would think a new principal would be comfortable with, and they definitely send a message that a small group of privileged kids are no longer running the show. . . . Here's one more dilemma. It seems for years this school has had a tradition of managing to figure out a way for the same group of kids, who come from the influential families in the neighborhood, to get most all of the awards, are selected as homecoming queen and king, give the speeches at graduation, and so on, and so on. How do you fix something that runs so deep . . . something so embedded in the culture?"

"If I hear you correctly, Brad, you're saying that there's been a double-standard for years, as the adults who run the school look the other way while kids of privilege are given their assumed place at the top of the pecking order. What a disappointing testament to how trained educators cave to the social injustice of small-town politics."

"Yes, you have assessed the reality very well, my good friend."

"Well, thinking out loud here, here's what I think I'd consider if I were that new principal. I'd work with my school council, and I'd appoint a new committee that represented a cross-section of the entire faculty and student body, and I'd give that team the charge of looking at *all* student recognition policies and procedures—top to bottom—senior class right on down through ninth grade. I'd ask this new team to research how awards and recognition are given, what kids and their accomplishments are somehow being left out, and to then bring their findings and recommendations back to the school council as soon as possible."

"Then I'd shore up the weak areas, where maybe staff are arbitrarily making decisions on who gets what. I'd send the new-and-improved philosophy and policy home in a newsletter, so every parent knew that the school is going to higher levels of social justice—with more kids being recognized and celebrated for their accomplishments. I'd make sure everyone in the school and community knew that this school was about "win, win," and *every* student—not just the few who have been born into privilege and affluence."

"Wow, John, you make it sound so clear and simple. . . . Who would not understand this paradigm shift?"

"It is simple, Brad—just takes some courage and a relentless refusal to bow down to past practices that have been hurting people. What principal, what teacher, what parent would not want the school to be so steeped in integrity? . . . Now, about that milkshake . . . I think I want a banana split and cheeseburger instead. What are we waiting on, son? Let's go!"

In Privileged Thinking in Today's Schools—The Implications for Social Justice, *David Barnett, Carol Christian, Richard Hughes, and Rocky Wallace (2010) dive deep under the surface in self-reflection, as they look back to various instances of social injustice that they realize now they allowed to take place on their watch as school administrators.*

SUMMARY

Brad seeks John's assistance in how to help a new principal address the harm that a clique of privileged students is causing his school. John gives sage advice on not only how to bust up the clique's influence, but also how to take the entire school to a higher level of integrity and celebration of every student's gifts and abilities.

REFLECTIONS

1. How do you deal with the pressure from influential parents who expect special treatment for their children?
2. Does your school have a fair and equitable student-assignment policy for all teachers and classes?
3. Have you ever witnessed a classroom or school held hostage by a group of kids who have learned how to control the system and live by different rules?

Chapter Nineteen

The "Goodness" Factor

When asked how her parents had raised such good kids, the oldest daughter simply replied: "Mom and Dad were just good people. They knew what was best for us, and they not only preached it, they lived it."

Life lesson: There are people in every community who by their good and honest lives establish the core values of the community. These are the precious souls you want on your staff, volunteering on your committees, having major influence on your school.

As the end of the school year approached, John had begun working on a book that outlined how to build a refreshing innovative school model. When Brad swung by one afternoon after school to talk about graduation, he found John immersed in his writing.

"All these years, Brad—I've wanted to do this. Your school clique issue helped me realize that it was time. I want to create a school model that is based on virtues and values—character ed, our forefathers and their intent, giving back to the community, classrooms that focus on creativity and critical thinking skills and kids breaking out of unhealthy cycles, school and learning as a lifestyle—not simply a "place," administrators not being drawn into "playing the game." At least those are the chapters I've finished first draft thus far."

"John, the principals in our network will love this! Wow, I can envision this resource being shared all across the country as time goes on."

"Not so fast, son. I'm not even halfway through it yet. Plus I'm not so sure enough folks in education these days do realize that this is the missing piece."

"But that's why you need to write it, John. . . . What is your working title?"

"I'm simply calling it, *The 'Goodness' Factor.* This is the cornerstone of how great schools will be developed in the future. Everything else we've tried has been the trim, and that's why we still see many schools failing. The key ingredient to taking school communities to new levels of effectiveness hinges on the 'heart' of the principal, and the heart of the teacher in the classroom."

"John, you have a winner here. I can't wait to read it. Could I take some sample chapters to read to the principal's cadre next time we meet?"

"Sure. I think they'd enjoy a discussion on why they went into this profession in the first place, and what they feel is missing."

"What are some of your other themes you're thinking about including?"

"Nothing I've not stressed before, Brad. You know what I strongly believe we have left out in our current school structures. Kids need stimulating classrooms, with an array of 'hands-on' experiences and technology. Kids need clubs, and field trips they'll never forget. They need intramurals, and quality physical education. They need to be immersed in 'the arts.' They need chorus and band, and guest entertainers to come to their school. As they get older, they need one-to-one mentoring and 'advisor/ advisee' small-group time. They need enough counselors on staff to truly help them navigate through the maze of college applications and scholarship opportunities. They need release time and adults who will take them to visit colleges and universities."

"And we are doing some of this, aren't we, John?"

"Yes, Brad, we are—here and there, in a scattered 'spray-and-pray' approach that is vastly inadequate for a society that is thirsting for school to be more than what worked in the past."

"Did it work that well, John?"

"For those from privileged homes who could navigate the game, Brad—it has worked pretty well. Yet, we still have embarrassing drop-out rates. We still have way too many college freshmen who just can't get the work done and thus quit school. We still have too many kids somehow thinking that even without skills and training society will create a job for them, or worse, take care of them. This is a mindset that is crippling our culture across the board, Brad. And it doesn't have to be this way."

"Brad, we have the know-how to truly invent mastery learning centers that can become a 'state-of-the-art' support system of well-adjusted, inspired movers and shakers who will leave their P–12 experience equipped to launch out into a bold new world of promise. But living and dying with assessment scores will not produce such a school. Accountability is part of the puzzle, certainly. But we've played that game for years, and it still leaves us wanting, and needing more in how we educate our children."

"Will the 'goodness' factor really change the way we approach our current schooling 'systems,' John? I mean, there are only so many ways we can structure school days, and master schedules, and course offerings, and sports, and so on."

"And that's been the problem all along, son. We have somehow been satisfied with a very limited set of paradigms on how we can provide school structures. Who says we cannot re-think how we use our time and resources to facilitate learning? Technology is the 'wild card'—totally changes everything."

John almost preached with passion. "And who says we can't offer a more varied menu of services? We have highly trained volunteers waiting in the wings—recreational enthusiasts, mathematicians, artists, musicians, authors, dance instructors, and other folks with special skills and passions who would love to coordinate clubs at school for kids that would go far beyond what we have the capacity to provide with our limited funding and staff ratios. When did we start thinking in such bureaucratic, narrow mindsets, Brad? John Dewey was calling for such a creative approach to schooling several decades ago."

"It just becomes a routine, I guess, John. Like any nine-to-five job, teachers become overloaded with the daily grind, and after a while, the comfort of the routine is what keeps them going."

"Then we must address this bent toward mediocrity, Brad! School cannot be routine—with its facilitators of knowledge buying into this assembly-line, factory mentality. Such a classroom culture bores our students right out of their minds. You know it. I know it. Everyone knows it. With the technology kids have access to today, and how much they love it, in many instances, they're coming to school and going through the motions—but the real learning kicks in after school when they go home to their life on the Internet. Do educators not get it? Do we not realize that 'school' as we now do it could become obsolete in less than ten years?! Or even five years?"

"I know, John. I know. You keep working on that book. It needs to be out there in the mainstream. We do seem to still not 'get it.' . . . Oh, I almost forgot what I came by to ask you. Would you feel up to giving our commencement address at Smithtown High School's graduation? I know of no one who can convey to kids what's really important in life better than you." Brad's voice broke, and he looked away.

"Brad, I'm inclined to say that my doctor would not agree to me attempting this. But let me talk to Marge about it. If we get the green light, I'll do it. And, I'm so honored to be invited to be on the stage for such an important 'rite of passage' for your seniors. I'll do my best to be there."

In Drive—The Surprising Truth about What Motivates Us, *Daniel Pink (2010) investigates the universal intrinsic thirst for creativity, and how empowering students and employees generates far more results than controlling and manipulating their work.*

SUMMARY

John realizes he needs to put his insights about school improvement on paper, and begins work on his first book. Brad visits John and gets an inside peek at the first draft, and sees that the potential of this project is limitless.

REFLECTIONS

1. In your school's efforts to improve, how much time do you spend on assessing how much staff relationships with students equates to their success?
2. How much does the "goodness" factor influence your school culture?
3. Does your school or district provide professional development for all staff in how to build trusting, genuine relationships with all stakeholders in the school community?

Chapter Twenty

What Really Matters

The old man was asked what he'd do differently, if he could live his life all over again. He smiled: "Oh my, I'd take my shoes off when the spring rains came and run through the grass like there was no tomorrow. Because now, there isn't."

Life lesson: Servant leaders walk the "road less traveled," and that makes all the difference.

John became weaker in the days leading up to graduation, and his doctor would not give the OK for him to deliver the commencement address. But he did write something for the seniors, and he asked Marge to represent him and read it. She stopped many times to compose herself, but she got through it as only a loving wife can. John's message to the kids he loved so much, simply called "Life," silenced the "house," and at the end, Margie finished by adding, "Seniors, you go for it! My husband told me to tell you to chase your dreams, and make this town proud! Every day, be a blessing."

Life

There are only so many snows on Christmas.
Mamaw and Papaw will not be here as long as you may assume.
A word spoken in anger is regretted sometimes for a lifetime.
Your brothers and sisters absolutely think you hung the moon.
They will never build a mall that can compare to a walk in the woods.
You will never find a substitute for your Mom's cooking.
Your classmates who are picked on at school—they love it when you say "hi" in the hall.
Your favorite teachers keep those "thank you" notes for a lifetime.
Family vacations to the ocean, or to the mountains—truly indeed almost Heaven.

Your pets really do wait all afternoon for you to get home from school.
Your class pictures will hang on these walls for a hundred years.
Your Dad brags on you at work, and carries your photograph wherever he goes.
Your smiles bring healing so much more than you know.
Your laughter is contagious, and can change the mood in a room.
Your pastor prays for you daily as you venture out beyond the walls of the church.
Your dreams are but a stone's throw away. . . . Chase them!
Your mind is God's gift to you. . . . Use it to make a difference in this world.
And on the rough days, remember your roots.
And on your mountaintop days, keep both feet on the ground.
Oh, my precious children, it all will go by so fast.
Cherish every day.
Cherish every relationship.
Jump in the mud puddles, and skip rocks on the pond.
Life is the journey. . . . Live it with passion, with goodness, with joy.
We are so proud of you, and all you have become.
Don't look down with fear.
Don't look back with regret.
Keep focused on the road He's given you—and walk it ever so well.
Always, always . . . be a blessing.

In Tipping Point, *Malcolm Gladwell (2002) demonstrates with a variety of examples how the little things make a big, big difference, emphasizing that one person can indeed turn the tide.*

Bonus Resources

SCHOOL CULTURE AUDIT

In our organization: Rate each from 1 to 10, and then tally the total.

1. Membership has an agreed-upon vision, believes in the vision, can quote the vision to others, and is focused on assisting in making the vision a reality.
2. Our organization is moving away from "top-down" decision making, and moving toward a flattened shared leadership model that has more people involved, encourages the sharing of new ideas, and is "restless" to move the organization from good to great.
3. Our organization has identified our core values, and has also provided training for members to identify and develop their personal core values.
4. In all team planning and decision-making meetings, the conversation is aligned with the organization's core values. The purpose of the meeting is to help the organization to rise to "smarter," more effective work.
5. We have a high level of trust in our organization.
6. We have effective accountability models in place on all levels of our organization (we allow no one to wander outside our agreed-upon organizational ethical boundaries).
7. Members of our organization enjoy being here, and the work culture is celebrative, "alive," "fun," and always in "think-tank" mode. We aren't afraid of thinking outside the box—we thrive on it.
8. Our executive leadership team is empowering and equipping of all others in the organization (as opposed to insecure and controlling).

9. We do not have toxic culture issues that are not handled with grace (we are not trapped in political correctness in regards to who has the clout and who has the power—thus leading to double standards in controversial or ethical situations).
10. We are about the health of the organization and how it serves the community and beyond, not the overprotection of individuals. Succession planning is in place on all levels of the organization.

(Rocky Wallace, Morehead State University, 2008)

SCHOOL DISTRICT AUDIT

Healthy culture is absolutely critical for any organization to be effective—and a place where people want to work, and other stakeholders trust and feel good about. Rate the overall culture in your school district. Rate on a scale of 1 to 10, and use the questions below to guide you in this informal self-assessment.

Organizational Culture Assessment (district-level audit):

1. Is our district a friendly place to visit (physical attractiveness, personable, professional customer service)?
2. Does each school (in general) have a good working climate (do staff like each other, trust each other, work well together)?
3. Do our schools trust our district office staff, and have good relationships with the district office and school board?
4. Does our designated leadership (principals, C/O directors, superintendent) empower and equip all staff (are new ideas and suggestions welcome, quality PD provided, staff in the trenches trusted to make the decisions needed to make their schools more effective)?
5. Does our district embrace the team decision-making approach? Are an abundance of teams trained and developed on the school level?
6. Do we go out of our way to ask for and listen to the suggestions of our parents?
7. Do we do "exit interviews" with our students as they leave elementary, middle, and high school? (Do we ask them how we could have made their experience better, what needs to stay, what needs to go, what needs to be adjusted, what needs to be added?)
8. Are we moving away from the "old school" days of political havoc and a few manipulating the entire school district?

9. Do we celebrate enough (student successes, staff successes, school and district awards, innovative programs recognized prominently in the community and across the region/state)?

10. Are we "letting go" of those practices, processes, structures, and strategies that no longer work very well (and are we embracing the new technologies, what we now know about how kids learn best, multiple intelligences, the need for a variety of clubs/other extracurricular and content opportunities for each child on all grade levels)?

11. Do we embrace and understand the "professional learning community" concept, with teachers/staff regularly meeting in small groups to discuss student work, and to make adjustments when students are not mastering the learning?

12. Are we addressing student bullying and harassment issues aggressively, and effectively?

13. Do we have effective advisor/advisee programs in place for our middle and high school students?

14. Do we require staff to do home visits in order to meet parents on their turf, and to build more trusting home-school relationships?

(Rocky Wallace, Morehead State University, 2008)

COMMON THEMES IN SCHOOL IMPROVEMENT EFFORTS

1. Advisor/advisee programs that meet a variety of cocurricular and noncurricular needs.

2. More variety of courses (less time spent on some—flexible, not rigid master schedules).

3. ACT prep and alignment of curricular offerings to better prepare students for college/other postsecondary.

4. More time at school for recess, other flexibility in the school day.

5. Art/music/PE focus increased, not decreased.

6. More clubs, intramurals, and other in-school and after-school opportunities.

7. Staff visiting other schools more to observe effective programs.

8. Students visiting college campuses more often and sooner.

9. More field trips, not fewer.

10. Technology interwoven into more courses.

11. Attention paid to the culture factor—relationships, relationships, relationships.

12. Increase in community partnerships and bringing in paraprofessionals or visiting specialists from outside education to speak to and work with students.
13. Staff IGPs that are "alive" and meaningful.
14. School safety focus, especially in the area of the subculture of bullying and harassment.
15. Student interviews/surveys utilized as a key part of the school's total process of data collection.

(Rocky Wallace, Morehead State University, 2009)

EFFECTIVE MODEL FOR LEADERSHIP TEAM DEVELOPMENT

Key Principles:

- Outside facilitators are an advantage.
- Core values of the organization need to be identified.
- Specific time needs to be set aside over a period of several months or longer.
- The team should meet in a protected location (free of distractions and the temptation to do work while simultaneously involved in the sessions).
- Titles are left at the door.
- Trust and transparency are essential.
- Book studies are a key strategy in available resources being utilized.
- Food, fun, a relaxed atmosphere are essential.
- Goals, vision, dreams are discussed.
- "Sacred cows" and paradigms that may no longer be helpful are challenged.
- Transformational change is not just hoped for, but expected.
- Participants are given plenty of time to tell their "stories."
- Self-leadership and growth are built into the process.
- Leadership/organizational health research is studied, and built into the process.
- Group members are actively involved in the learning (skits, presentations, etc.).
- Effective teamwork principles are modeled.
- If the group is large, some follow-up sessions may include smaller group work.
- The concept of "incubator" is fiercely protected—meaning that participants are being carefully shepherded and coached while the group grows into something healthier, stronger, and more effective.

- Sarcasm and negativity are not allowed in the group dynamics—although honest discussion is an ongoing part of the process.
- Participants will come away with the ability to then lead another group through the process, thus allowing the model and its effectiveness to multiply to the larger organization, or other organizations.

(Rocky Wallace, Morehead State University, 2009)

THE PRINCIPAL'S WHEEL

The principal who lives servant leadership will invest in, and have influence on an array of other stakeholders. This graphic illustrates the tremendous responsibility that falls on the shoulders of a school principal.

Summary of Current Values-Based Leadership Research

- Leadership is intricately linked to character, integrity, and ethics.
- Authentic leadership is values-driven, and focuses on serving.
- Many leaders have a unique humility that often shifts the credit to others.
- A leader's emotional intelligence—how well he or she listens, communicates, praises, inspires—is key to his or her effectiveness.
- A leader's core values eventually help define the organization as well, and will be the deciding factor in how well he moves the organization from success to significance.
- Leaders, although realizing and supporting the organization's need for positive change, are routinely resistant to change themselves.
- Leaders often find it hard to equip, empower, and then trust their people.
- There is a dark side of leadership that makes all leaders vulnerable to unhealthy control and insecurity tendencies, and ethical blind spots. If unable to look in the mirror and make the necessary changes, the leader in denial of his weak areas will eventually crash and burn, or lose credibility.
- The only person a leader can really change is himself.
- Developing quality mentoring programs for staff is a key strategy in building the strongest team possible.
- Not all employees are the same. Each have unique personalities, talents, and tendencies. Thus, individual treatment of each person, and meeting their developmental needs, is key in more employees being content and loyal to the organization for longer periods of time.
- Culture is a critical piece in an organization's effectiveness, and in creating a positive, celebrative, and trusting work climate. The leader sets the tone.
- Ethics are ethics. There are no "shortcuts" that can be rationalized as "OK in that situation". That mindset has brought down many large and powerful organizations that seemed immune to ethical and legal scrutiny.
- Helping employees to find their niche—where they work best and are inspired-- separates the good organizations from the average ones.
- Not accepting just being good is what separates the great from the rest.
- A focus on relationships, not pre-occupation with data and profit, is key. Relationships prioritized first produce the profits long term. A leader's greatest resources are his people.
- In determining how to strategically plan, how to move forward, a leader is wise to identify personal and organizational core values. Core values are what drives everything else—24/7. An organization's core values can be felt by a visitor as he walks through the corporate offices.
- Leadership is not about controlling people—it is about caring for people.
- Taking risks, making mistakes, apologizing, taking responsibility for something that didn't turn out well—all a daily part of the job for the servant leader.
- Leaders have a vision for the future of their organization, and lay the groundwork for uninterrupted success after they leave.

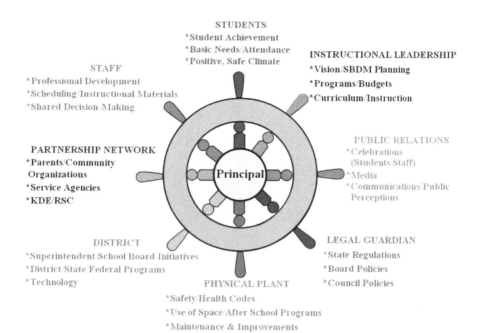

STUDENTS
*Student Achievement
*Basic Needs/Attendance
*Positive, Safe Climate

INSTRUCTIONAL LEADERSHIP
*Vision/SBDM Planning
*Programs/Budgets
*Curriculum/Instruction

STAFF
*Professional Development
*Scheduling/Instructional Materials
*Shared Decision-Making

PUBLIC RELATIONS
*Celebrations
(Students/Staff)
*Media
*Communications/Public
Perceptions

PARTNERSHIP NETWORK
*Parents/Community
Organizations
*Service Agencies
*KDE/RSC

DISTRICT
*Superintendent/School Board Initiatives
*District/State Federal Programs
*Technology

LEGAL GUARDIAN
*State Regulations
*Board Policies
*Council Policies

PHYSICAL PLANT
*Safety/Health Codes
*Use of Space/After School Programs
*Maintenance & Improvements

The Principal's Wheel

References

Abrashoff, D. M. (2002). *It's Your Ship.* New York: Warner Books.

Babauta, L. (2009). *The Power of Less.* New York: Hyperion.

Barnett, D., C. Christian, R. Hughes, and R. Wallace. (2010). *Privileged Thinking in Today's Schools.* Lanham, MD: Rowman & Littlefield Education.

Blanchard, K. (1999). *The Heart of a Leader.* Colorado Springs, CO: Honor Books.

Buford, B. (1994). *Halftime.* Grand Rapids, MI: Zondervan.

Citrin, J. M., and R. A. Smith. (2003). *The Five Patterns of Extraordinary Careers.* New York: Crown Business.

Cloud, H. (2004). *9 Things You Simply Must Do.* Nashville: Integrity Publishers.

Conners, N. A. (2000). *If You Don't Feed the Teachers They Eat the Students!* Nashville: Incentive Publications.

Daniels, H., and M. Bizar. (1998). *Methods That Matter.* York, Maine: Stanhouse Publishers.

Gladwell, M. (2002). *The Tipping Point.* New York: Little, Brown, and Company.

Gregory, G. H., and C. Chapman. (2002). *Differentiated Instructional Strategies.* Thousand Oaks, CA: Corwin Press.

Harvard Business School. (2004). *Teams That Succeed.* Boston: Harvard Business School Press.

Lennick, D., and F. Kiel. (2008). *Moral Intelligence.* University of Pennsylvania: Wharton.

Maxwell, J. C. (2000). *Failing Forward.* Nashville: Thomas Nelson.

Maxwell, J. C. (2008). *Leadership Gold.* Nashville: Thomas Nelson.

Middleton, K. E., and E. A. Pettitt. (2007). *Who Cares?* Tucson, AZ: Wheatmark.

Morgan, G. (1997). *Imaginization.* San Francisco: Barrett-Koehler.

Pink, D. (2010). *Drive.* New York: Riverhead Books.

Rothwell, W. J. (2005). *Effective Succession Planning.* New York: Amacom.

Tushman, M. L., and C. A. O'Reilly. (2002). *Winning Through Innovation.* Boston: Harvard Business School Press.

SUGGESTED FURTHER READING

City, E. A., R. F. Elmore, S. E. Fiarman, and L.Teitel. (2009). *Instructional Rounds in Education.* Cambridge, MA: Harvard Education Press.

DuFour, R., R. DuFour, and R. Eaker. (2008). *Revisiting Professional Learning Communities at Work.* Bloomington, IN: Solution Tree Press.

Fullan, M. (2011). *The Moral Imperative Realized.* Thousand Oaks, CA: Corwin.

Green, R. L. (2010). *The Four Dimensions of Principal Leadership.* Boston: Pearson.

Hargreaves, A., and M. Fullan, eds. (2009). *Change Wars.* Bloomington, IN: Solution Tree Press.

Houston, P. D., and S. L. Sokolow. (2006). *The Spiritual Dimension of Leadership.* Thousand Oaks, CA: Corwin.

Jacobs, H. H. (2010). *Curriculum 21.* Alexandria, VA: ASCD.

Parkay, F. W., G. Hass, and E. J. Anctil. (2010). *Curriculum Leadership,* 9th ed. Boston: Allyn and Bacon.

Pollock, J. E., and S. M. Ford. (2009). *Improving Student Learning One Principal at a Time.* Alexandria, VA: ASCD.

Reeves, D. B. (2009). *Leading Change in Your School.* Alexandria, VA: ASCD.

Stein, S. J., and L. Gewirtzman. (2003). *Principal Training on the Ground.* Portsmouth, NH: Heinemann.

Tishman, S., D. N. Perkins, and E. Jay. (1995). *The Thinking Classroom.* Needham Heights, MA: Allyn and Bacon.

Tomlinson, C. A., K. Brimijoin, and L. Narvaez. (2008). *The Differentiated School.* Alexandria, VA: ASCD.

Whitaker, T. *What Great Principals Do Differently.* Larchmont, NY: Eye On Education.

About the Author

Rocky Wallace teaches graduate classes in instructional leadership and writes leadership curriculum, serving as coordinator of the Principal Program and assistant professor of graduate education at Asbury University. As a former principal, he writes his articles and books from the unique perspective of the practitioner down in the trenches, and has had three previous books published by Rowman & Littlefield Education on the role the principal plays in school improvement. He has also coauthored two other books that address the critical importance of teacher/student relationships, and school culture.

While Wallace was principal at Catlettsburg Elementary in Boyd County, Kentucky, the school was named a Kentucky and U.S. Blue Ribbon School in 1996–1997. He began his administrative career while serving as principal at Fallsburg School, a P–8 center in Lawrence County, Kentucky (his home county, where he was born and raised).

As he moved on to leadership consulting work with the Kentucky Department of Education in 2000, and later as director of Instructional Support at the Kentucky Educational Development Corporation in Ashland, Kentucky, Wallace realized that school principals of this generation face a perplexing dilemma: they are being asked to do more and more in turning our nation's educational system around, but too often without the needed support of caring and experienced mentors who have been principals themselves.

While studying strategic leadership as he completed his doctoral work at Regent University in Virginia Beach, Virginia, Wallace realized that the answer in how to create more effective schools that focus on the holistic needs of children and youth is in embracing the principles of servant leadership. Thus, the core value of "serving" and putting people over profit, while addressing key organizational culture issues, is found throughout his writing.

Wallace received his undergraduate degree from Berea College in 1979 and his MA from Morehead State in 1983. He is married to Denise, who is the Christian education director at Carlisle United Methodist Church in Nicholas County, Kentucky, where the couple share pastoral duties. The Wallaces have two daughters, Lauren (husband, Ely) and Bethany, and live on a small farm outside of Winchester, Kentucky. Wallace has also provided consulting support to other education agencies, and assists Morehead State University in an adjunct role with its doctoral program in educational leadership. His hobbies include enjoying the outdoors and traveling with his family.

CPSIA information can be obtained
at www.ICGtesting.com
Printed in the USA
LVHW090207060320
649194LV00001B/79